# THE TALMUD
# FOR BEGINNERS

# THE TALMUD FOR BEGINNERS

### Volume 2

## Text

Judith Z. Abrams

JASON ARONSON INC.
*Northvale, New Jersey*
*London*

The author gratefully acknowledges permission to reprint from the following sources:

From *Midrash on Psalms,* translated by William G. Braude. Copyright © 1959 by Yale University Press. Copyright © renewed 1987 by William G. Braude. Reprint permission granted by Yale University Press.

From *The Talmud: The Steinsaltz Edition,* by Adin Steinsaltz. Copyright © 1983 by Israel Institute for Talmudic Publications. Reprint permission granted by Adin Steinsaltz and Israel Institute for Talmudic Publications.

**Library of Congress Cataloging-in-Publication Data**

Abrams, Judith Z.
  The Talmud for beginners.

  Includes bibliographical references (p. 195–198) and indexes.
    Contents: v. 1. Prayer — v. 2. Text.
    1. Talmud—Introductions.  I. Title.
BM503.5.A27  1991     296.1′2061     90-1211
ISBN 0-87668-734-6 (set)
ISBN 0-87668-719-2 (v. 1) (hb)
ISBN 1-56821-022-1 (v. 1) (pb)
ISBN 0-87668-597-1 (v. 2) (pb)

Manufactured in the United States of America. Jason Aronson Inc. offers books and cassettes. For information and catalog write to Jason Aronson Inc., 230 Livingston Street, Northvale, New Jersey 07647.

"Commemorate me for generations." —*Megillah* 7a

For my family's matriarchs:
Gramma
Aunt Sonia
Mom
Aunt Thea
and
Shirley

# Contents

# Preface

When I decided to present the tractate *Megillah* in this second volume of *Talmud for Beginners,* I thought it would be much easier for people to learn, compared with the material in tractate *Berachot. Berachot* dealt with practical issues of prayer: when to say the *Shema,* how to say the *Amidah,* and the like. I thought the reasoning behind such practical decisions would be difficult to understand, compared to the less tangible matters addressed in *Megillah. Megillah* is full of *midrash,* expositions on the biblical text, which I thought would be easier to study. I was wrong. In teaching this material, I discovered that the midrashic process was a challenge for people to understand. It is full of free associations and unvoiced values and assumptions that are far from our experience of life and Judaism today.

In the process of learning the midrashic method, you may ask yourself "Why learn *midrash?*" There are two reasons that learning the midrashic method is important. One, because it is a large part of the way the rabbis think. And two, it shows you how to delve into the text of the *Tanach* for yourself. It is quite challenging, but it is worth it. Just remember to read each passage out loud and go slowly. Allow yourself time to understand each passage before you move on to the next one. You may find it helpful to read the Book of Esther before you begin this book. Also, you will probably want to have a *Tanach,* a Jewish Bible, handy as you read, as well as a traditional prayer book.

Holiness is a combination of text, time, and people. I have been blessed to have many people help me as I studied the text of this tractate. Dr. Avraham Amir of Ben Gurion University in Beer Sheva, Israel, helped me immensely in my studies of Talmud. Rabbi Joseph Radinsky of United Orthodox Synagogues, my Talmud teacher, guided me in my interpretation of the *sugyot* presented here. Dr. David Kraemer of The Jewish Theological Seminary also provided me with guidance and helpful comments. Larry Washington, Beth Schwartz, David Gilbert, Thea Cooper, and Dr. Lucy Zabarenko read over this manuscript and made many helpful suggestions. In addition, my Talmud class at Congregation Ner Shalom, in Woodbridge, Virginia—attended by Brie Barclay, Faith Barclay, Amy Gerver, Michelle Rendelman, Bob Schneider, Shirley Udelson, Larry Washington, and Leah Washington—and my Confirmation class there—attended by Amy M. Hardison, Michelle L. Hummel, Lisa Leon, Joseph K. Mintzer, Larry Newdorf, Matthew Rich, Lecia P. Slater, and Leah M. Washington—all helped me a great deal in understanding the text. Truly, I have learned much from my teachers, more from my colleagues, and most from my students.

I would also like to thank Arthur Kurzweil of Jason Aronson for giving me this opportunity, and Muriel Jorgenson for doing such a fine job of editing. Thanks to Rabbi Jason Z. Edelstein for his spiritual guidance. And finally, thanks to my loving husband, Steven, my son, Michael, and my daughter, Ruth. They make everything I do possible and worthwhile.

# Introduction

O ne of the most enjoyable moments I have had as a rabbi was a wedding ceremony I performed for a couple on their fiftieth wedding anniversary. In 1939, the man and woman both fled Germany by different routes but ended up together in Holland for a short time. There they were hastily married in a civil ceremony, after which they both fled Europe. They eventually settled in this country, raised their children, and supported their synagogue, but never had a Jewish wedding. For their fiftieth anniversary, their children decided to put on a wedding for them, complete with flowers, *chuppah* (Jewish wedding canopy), reception, cake – the works. What a pleasure to plan this wedding with the couple, explain the traditions to them, and talk with them about their fifty years together! After all, at how many weddings does a rabbi officiate knowing that the marriage will last fifty years? We settled many details, including the decision to use a beautiful, illuminated, egalitarian *ketubah* (Jewish wedding contract).

The night of the wedding came. The groom came down the aisle first, stood under the *chuppah,* and looked down the aisle as his bride approached in a lavender dress. They were both surprisingly nervous. We repeated the ancient blessings and then I had each party repeat after me the vows written in the *ketubah.* I said to the groom, "Repeat after me. I shall treasure you."

"I shall treasure you," he repeated, looking at his wife.

"nourish you"

"nourish you"

"support you"

"support you"

"and respect you"

"and respect you," he said. As he said that last phrase, his wife wagged a finger at him and shot him a meaningful glance that said as clearly as words, "Ha! Now I've got you. *That's* what I wanted!" It was so spontaneous, and so bespoke what she really wanted, that we all broke out laughing.

That moment embodied a basic truth. All the love and affection in the world do not make up for even a small amount of respect. Being respected—that is, being listened to, understood, and valued—are worth a great deal, not only to us as people, but to the texts we treasure as Jews.

It is exactly this concept of respect or honor, and the ways we show it, that is the subject of this tractate, *Megillah*, the Scroll. Honor, *Kavod*, in relation to our sacred texts, is the organizing principle and main topic of this tractate. It is quite fitting that the topic of honor is suggested by the story of Esther, for honor, and the desire for it, is the linchpin of her tale. The *Megillah's* story is a tale filled with honor and duty. Esther, a Jewish woman, marries the king of Persia, Ahashueros, whom some identify as Xerxes (486–465 B.C.E.). While she is in the king's palace her guardian, Mordecai, learns of a plot to kill the king and foils it. Now, Ahashueros's advisor, Haman, disliked Mordecai and intended to have him killed. However, before Haman can accomplish his evil plan, the king learns that Mordecai has protected him from death, and Ahashueros showers Mordecai with honors. This makes Haman quite angry, and he vows to kill all the Jews. Esther, through courage and daring, informs the king of this plot, and Haman and his family are killed instead of the Jews. Honor plays a crucial role in this story. If Haman had not wanted honor so badly, he might not have hatched his plot to be rid of the Jews.

Unlike tractate *Berachot*, which is tightly organized using many different dimensions, this tractate appears to be much more loosely structured. Instead of progressing in a linear fashion through the chronology of a day, or according to what occurs more and less frequently, this tractate seems to be organized in a pattern of concentric circles. The tractate starts with the very core of holiness, the internalization of Torah, and moves in ever-expanding circles from that center. The first chapter deals with the reading of the text of Scripture itself, using the *Megillah* as its example, showing us how to study it, internalize it, and so merit honor for ourselves. The second chapter deals with the reading of text, such as the *Megillah* or the Torah, as a ritual act, for example, reading the Torah in synagogue on Mondays, Thursdays, and Shabbat and reading the Scroll of Esther on Purim, and so forth. The third chapter deals with the way we show honor to the essence of Torah within the synagogue. Finally, the fourth chapter examines the interaction of Torah and honor with the world at large. This "concentric circles" organization moves from the most intense, private, and elevated experience of text to the most public and, perhaps, diffuse experience of Torah and honor. (This is the exact *opposite* order in which most people encounter God's presence when they make their own spiritual journeys. We usually begin seeking God in the everyday world, which leads us to the synagogue, which leads us to practice Judaism and finally to direct, intense contact with God through the text.) The source of all the honor regulated in this system is the process of taking Torah, God's word and essence, into ourselves.

There are many beautiful spiritual consequences that result from the rabbis' basing their system of honor on Torah. This system had a desirable impact on the lives of the Jews for whom it was prescribed. Systems of political and military honor in the secular world were often closed to Jews. The system of honoring the Torah learned by a person provided a status system that could be internally controlled, used, and recognized within the Jewish community when routes to honor in the outside world were closed.

Before we embark on a study of this tractate, we should explore how this document developed. Please note that while there are many hotly debated theories as to how the Mishnah and Gemara were created, you will be provided here with a relatively traditional explanation. However, much interesting material has been written on this subject. You will find suggestions for further reading on this topic in the back of this book. The Talmud is called the Oral Torah. Tradition has it that God whispered the laws and customs contained in this Torah to Moses on Mount Sinai at the same time God gave Moses the Written Torah (the first five books of the Bible). According to *Pirkei Avot* 1:1, this Oral Torah was passed down through the generations, "from Moses to Joshua; Joshua to the elders; the elders to the prophets; and the prophets handed it down to the men of the Great Assembly."

These "men of the Great Assembly," who governed from approximately 500–200 B.C.E., were followed by *zugot*, pairs of leaders. (We should note here that some historians do not believe the Men of the Great Assembly ever existed.) Each *zug*, each pair, was composed of a *Nasi*, the President, and an *Av Beit Din*, the vice president. The *zugot* presided over the Sanhedrin, the Jewish judicial and legislative body of the era. As in any political body, different factions fought for power. The main combatants of this era were the Sadducees, who believed only in the Written Torah, not in the Oral one, as did the Pharisees. The Sadducees tended to be of a wealthier economic class than the adherents of the Pharisees. As often happens, the wealthy were also politically conservative. In addition, they seem to have been more closely linked to the priests, an aristocratic class that ran the Temple cult in Jerusalem, than were the Pharisees. The Sadducees seem to fade from history after the destruction of the Temple by the Romans in 70 C.E. The last of the *zugot* were two teachers named Hillel and Shammai, around whom schools of thought formed. These two schools existed from the end of the first century B.C.E. until the beginning of the second century C.E. The members of Beit Shammai and Beit Hillel were all Pharisees, yet they had very different approaches to the law and life.

After the destruction of the Temple in 70 C.E. and the dispersion of the Jews from the Land of Israel, the Pharisees (now called *Tannaim*), who led the Jewish people, had to devise a form of Judaism that could survive this tragedy. The Temple and its sacrifices, which had been the core of Jewish worship, were destroyed. The Sanhedrin, as it functioned in Temple times, was gone. There was no central authority to unify Jewish practice throughout the Jews' wide dispersion. Different teachers in different cities taught their own individual traditions. Judaism threatened to disintegrate into small sects whose practices bore little relationship to one another. Something had to be done.

One of the greatest Jewish teachers, Rabbi Akiba, took the situation in hand and began to organize the different teachings of individual rabbis. (This material is summarized on *Sanhedrin* 86a.) This material that Rabbi Akiba helped organize became the *Mishnah*, the *Tosefta* (a collection of Tannaitic material that expands the themes found in the *Mishnah*), *Sifrah* (a *midrash* on the Book of Leviticus), and *Sifrei* (a *midrash* on most of the Book of Numbers and the Book of Deuteronomy). Rabbi Judah HaNasi completed the work of sorting through the different legal traditions taught in Judaism and compiled an authoritative body of Jewish teaching which is known as the *Mishnah*. When Rabbi Judah HaNasi felt that a certain tradition accurately reflected normative Jewish practice and thought, he included it in the *Mishnah* anonymously, without saying which rabbi taught the tradition. When an opinion was important or interesting but was not the opinion of the majority of rabbis, he attributed it to the rabbi who taught it. To understand the attributions seen so frequently in the Talmud, just imagine the difference it makes when a spokesperson says, "I am speaking in the name of the president (or the pope or the Queen of England)." Knowing something about the person who makes a statement helps us evaluate that statement's content. In general, an anonymous opinion is adopted as the law over one that is attributed to an individual rabbi. We may also state that, generally, those opinions stated last in a mishnah become law.

Rabbi Judah HaNasi, often called simply Rabbi, completed this work around 200 C.E. Those traditions that he included in his work became known as *mishnayot*. Those that he did not include became known as *baraitot*. Often, *baraitot* and *toseftot* (the plural of *tosefta*)—are cited by the *Amoraim*, the rabbis who wrote the Gemara, the commentary on the Mishnah. The *Mishnah* and *Gemara* together form the Talmud.

How were the different midrashim and collections of *mishnayot* used to compose the Talmud? To understand how this came about, we must imagine we are sitting in an ancient academy when a question of Jewish practice is taken up. The head of the academy, the *Rosh Yeshivah*, would sit and listen as his *Amora* (also known as the *Meturgeman*, the Translator), a kind of "*Rosh Yeshivah* in training" would lead a discussion. When this *Amora* had learned enough, he could eventually become a *Rosh Yeshivah* himself. Before the *Rosh Yeshivah* and the *Amora* sat seven rows of sages, called *Chachamim*, "Wise ones." Behind them sat ten rows of students of the sages, called *Talmidei Chachamim*, "Students of the Wise Ones." On either side of these rows of *Chachamim* and *Talmidei Chachamim* sat *Tannaim*, literally, "Repeaters"—persons who knew the *mishnayot* of different schools by heart. These *Tannaim* had phenomenal memories and were like living books. They were allowed to repeat traditions but not interpret them. Around all these people sat the public, including women, who listened to the teachings of the sages. Finally, behind the *Rosh Yeshivah* and the *Amora*, but before the public, was a row designated for the *Nesiut*, the leaders of the community who did not know enough of the tradition to merit a seat among the *Chachamim*, the *Talmidei Chachamim*, or the *Tannaim*, but were too important to merely sit among the public.

When the sages would discuss a subject, they would first listen to the *mishnah* of Rabbi Yehuda HaNasi—the *Mishnah*, as we know it today—recited by a *Tanna*. Then the *Amora* would ask if any of the *Tannaim* knew any other material concerning the topic at hand that had been taught in the different schools (that is, *baraitot*), such as the material in the *Tosefta*. The *Tannaim* would recite the relevant material, and then the sages would begin their discussion with all the necessary prerequisite materials at hand.

Sometimes, as the rabbis discussed the *mishnah*, they would define it or discuss it in such a way that their interpretation of that *mishnah* became the accepted one—even if it contradicted the *mishnah*. In addition, the rabbis of the *Gemara* sometimes chose to emphasize certain *mishnayot* and not others. In this way, they were able to shape the impact the *mishnah* had on Jewish life. We see *Mishnah* through their eyes. It can be likened to this married couple: One partner is very quiet, and the other is quite talkative. The first partner might say a sentence, and then the second would chime in, saying, "Let me tell you what that meant." What the listener ends up hearing is the second partner's version of what the first partner meant. Usually the second partner is an accurate transmitter, but sometimes this partner inserts his or her own agenda into the first partner's words. The first partner here is the *Mishnah*. The second partner is the *Gemara*.

The men who participated in these discussions had different titles. The teachers whose work is preserved in the *Mishnah* are called *Tannaim*. Many of them had the title rabbi, which means "my teacher." Rabbis received their titles through ordination in the Land of Israel. Descendants of Hillel served as the *Nasi* by hereditary right, and their title was *Rabban*. The sages who discussed the *Mishnah* and composed the discussions found in the *Gemara* were known as *Amoraim* (those who taught from approximately 200–500 C.E.). The scholars of the Babylonian Talmud were not ordained rabbis and gave themselves such titles as *Rav* (master) or *Mar* (mister) — more lowly than the titles Rabbi and *Rabban* bestowed on the teachers in Palestine. All of the *Tannaim* lived in Palestine. Some of the *Amoraim* lived there, too, while other *Amoraim* resided in Babylonia. The sages who followed the *Amoraim* in the period from approximately 500–600 C.E. (and some say, up to 800 C.E.) in Babylonia are called *Saboraim*, or *Stamaim*. It is their finished product that we have in our hands today. In this volume, the authorities of both the *Mishnah* and the *Gemara* will be referred to as "the rabbis."

*Gemara* was written in two places: the Land of Israel and Babylonia. The one written in the Land of Israel is called the *Yerushalmi*, and was finished in approximately 400 C.E.; the other is the Babylonian Talmud, or *Bavli*, which was finished in approximately 500 C.E. Even though the Land of Israel had been the Jewish national homeland and the birthplace of the *Mishnah*, the Talmud produced there is less well known and less authoritative than the Babylonian Talmud, which ultimately became the Talmud used to guide everyday life.

Before we proceed to the text of this tractate itself, which is a record of the discussions and lessons described above, it will be helpful to understand how the rabbis approach the biblical text, what they do to it, and how. The rabbis believed that not one word in the *Tanach* is superfluous or erroneously written. Therefore, when a word might appear to be erroneously written, or superfluous, they assume it is there to teach us something, and they set out to find that hidden meaning. (However, even for the rabbis some sections of the *Tanach* were difficult to interpret, as we will see in Chapters 1 and 3.)

The rabbis also believed that they belonged to a consistent, reliable chain of tradition, dating all the way back to Moses and the forty years the Jewish people spent wandering in the desert. For them, the origin of almost everything in Judaism could be traced back to this period. If something appeared to be an innovation, they would find its origin in that ancient period and then deduce that this tradition had been forgotten and then revived, and thus only *looked* like an innovation. Of course, one might speculate that this was simply the rabbis *attributing* their own innovations to an earlier, holier, more authoritative generation.

Almost all of the rabbis' teachings stem from the text of Scriptures. Their basic, multilayered system of interpretation is called *Pardes*. It explores the texts on four levels: *Peshat* (the simple meaning of the text), *Remez* (the meaning that the text only hints at), *Drash* (the meaning expounded through *midrash*), and *Sod* (the secret, mystical meaning of the text). The first letter of each of these four levels spells the word *Pardes*—Orchard, or Paradise.

The *Peshat*, the simple meaning of the text, may lead to many interpretations. What is plain to one reader may seem different to another. For example, if the text says, "Behold, the bush burned with fire, and the bush was not consumed" (Exodus 3:2), one person may understand this verse to refer to one species of bush, and someone else will understand another species. So even the level of *peshat* speaks in many tongues.

*Remez* is the interpretation of Scriptures achieved through hints, puns, literary allusions, and numerology. Just as Roman letters are also numerals, so Hebrew letters have numerical values. While the rabbis related words and phrases that had the same numerical values, they did not deduce *halachot*, laws, by this method. The volume *The Spice of Torah Gymmatria* by

Gutman G. Locks is an invaluable aid in searching out these hinted-at meanings. This technique of text interpretation is utilized in this tractate. The following is a list of the numerical values of the Hebrew letters of the alphabet:

| | | |
|---|---|---|
| א *aleph* = 1 | ט *tet* = 9 | פ *pey* = 80 |
| ב *bet* = 2 | י *yud* = 10 | צ *tsadi* = 90 |
| ג *gimel* = 3 | כ *caf* = 20 | ק *kuf* = 100 |
| ד *dalet* = 4 | ל *lamed* = 30 | ר *reish* = 200 |
| ה *hey* = 5 | מ *mem* = 40 | ש *shin* = 300 |
| ו *vav* = 6 | נ *nun* = 50 | ת *tav* = 400 |
| ז *zayin* = 7 | ס *samech* = 60 | |
| ח *chet* = 8 | ע *ayin* = 70 | |

Thus, for example, the letters of the word *chai* (life)—*chet* and *yud*—add up to eighteen. The number 613 would be spelled *tav-reish-yud-gimel*. Sometimes numbers, such as this one, become used as words. Thus, these letters are pronounced *taryag* in the phrase *taryag mitzvot*, the 613 commandments.

The level of *Drash* is the exposition of the biblical text according to the Oral Tradition. This is a sophisticated system of interpretation that uses technical rules of interpretation of the *Tanach*, called hermeneutical rules. These rules were considered so important to Judaism that their recitation was made part of the morning prayer service. For example, the first of these rules permits us to deduce a major premise from a minor one. In Hebrew, this is called *kal vachomer*—literally, "light and weighty"—and is one of the most important methods of rabbinic textual interpretation. For example, a simple *kal vachomer* might run as follows: If it is good for a pitcher to pitch a strike, *kal vachomer*, all the more so is it good for him to pitch three strikes and strike the batter out.

The rabbis are not necessarily, nor even probably, looking only for the simple meaning *(peshat)* when they explicate a verse. They are trying to understand that verse in terms of their world and their relationship with God. Often they may try to solve the problems of their own day through their interpretations of ancient biblical verses. Not surprisingly, this often means that their interpretations have little to do with the simple meaning of the text. That doesn't make them less valuable; it just means we have to understand the rabbis' comments in their own context.

The rabbis often use texts from the *Tanach* to prove points they are making. This method of proving a point by using a verse from Scripture as proof or support is called proof texting. This exercise of proof texting often involves the use of verses out of their original context and in ways that may appear inconsistent with their meaning within the *Tanach* text.

This use of proof texts may make modern readers feel uncomfortable, particularly because this technique has been used by some non-Jewish expositors of Jewish texts to prove points of view not consistent with Judaism. The best known example may be the Christian interpretation of Isaiah 7:14, which states, "A young woman is with child and she will bear a son and will call him Immanu El." In its context, this verse refers to a situation that occurred centuries before Jesus was born. However, some Christian interpreters assert that it predicts the birth of Jesus. In doing so, they are using this verse as a proof text.

We need not feel uncomfortable about using a genuinely valuable method of interpretation just because it has been used by others for ends that do not further Judaism. On the contrary, how better to show the correct use of the *midrash* than to employ it ourselves? We may use this method to find meanings in the text that are consistent with our tradition yet speak to our contemporary situation.

Sometimes the proof texts the rabbis use may seem not to prove their point. Often this is because the "proof" can best be understood in the Hebrew or comes in the second half of the verse, although the rabbis only quote the first half. (They assumed you'd know the end of the verse and did not cite it.) Therefore, it is very important to look up these verses in context, and in Hebrew if possible, to understand the beauty and intricacy of the midrashim.

The level of *Sod*—the secret, mystical meaning of the text— is the deepest one we know. This form of study shows the inner connections between verses, words, letters, and eternal principles and attributes of God. Traditionally, this level of

Torah study is not engaged in publicly. The mystical teachings of this level of Torah interpretation are contained in the *Zohar*, a text of Jewish mysticism.

The rabbis used all the expositional methods at their disposal to interpret the story of Esther in ways that were meaningful and helpful to their listeners. They saw in Esther's story yet another battle between God's forces (Esther and Mordecai) and Israel's eternal enemy: Amalek and his descendants, among whose number Haman is included. Esther 3:1 ties Haman to Amalek through his father, Hammedata the Agagite (Agag was an Amalekite). Esther 2:5 ties Mordecai to Saul, the first king of Israel, through the following genealogy: "Mordecai, the son of Yair, the son of Shimi, the son of Kish, a Benjaminite." Saul was also a son of Kish from the tribe of Benjamin (1 Samuel 9:1, 21), who battled with the descendants of Amalekites (see 1 Samuel 15:1–35).

The Jewish people first met Amalek and his destructive force just after they became a people, in their first wandering in the desert after their liberation from slavery. Just after they had passed through the Red Sea and settled into a routine of eating manna, Amalek suddenly swooped down on them (Exodus 17:8–16).

> Then came Amalek and fought with Israel in Refidim. And Moses said to Joshua, "Choose us out men, and go out, fight with Amalek. Tomorrow I will stand on the top of the hill with the rod of God in my hand." So Joshua did as Moses had said to him, and fought with Amalek. And Moses, Aaron and Hur went up to the top of the hill. And it came to pass, when Moses held up his hand, that Israel prevailed, and when he let down his hand, Amalek prevailed. But Moses' hands were heavy, and they took a stone, and put it under him, and he sat on it. And Aaron and Hur supported his hands, the one on the one side, and the other on the other side, and his hands were steady until the going down of the sun. And Joshua harried Amalek and his people with the edge of the sword.
>
> And the Lord said to Moses, "Write this for a memorial in a book, and rehearse it in the ears of Joshua, that I will utterly blot out the remembrance of Amalek from under the heaven." And Moses built an altar, and called the name of it Adonai Nissi (the

Lord is my Banner) for he said, "Because the Lord has sworn by his throne that the Lord will have war with Amalek from generation to generation."

This senseless attack on the Jewish people had a great impact on our collective memory, for Moses mentions it again in one of his last speeches before he dies (Deuteronomy 25:17–19):

> Remember what Amalek did to you by the way, when you came out of Egypt. How he met you by the way and smote the hindmost of you, all that were feeble in your rear, when you were faint and weary. And he feared not God. Therefore it shall be, when the Lord your God has given you rest from all your enemies round about, in the land which the Lord your God gives you for an inheritance to possess it, that you shall blot out the remembrance of Amalek from under the heaven. You shall not forget.

This passage is read as the *maftir*, the extra portion between the Torah and *Haftarah* readings, on the *Shabbat* before Purim. This Sabbath is called *Shabbat Zachor*, the Sabbath of Remembrance, because of this portion. Thus, the rabbis frame the lighthearted festival of Purim against the background of the eternal war between good and evil.

These passages also serve as the origin for the custom of making noise on Purim. We are commanded to blot out – literally erase – the remembrance of Amalek. Therefore, Jews would write the name Amalek on their shoes in chalk, and when Haman's name was read in the *Megillah*, they would stamp their feet, wiping out his, and his ancestor's, name.

It is most interesting that the rabbis felt we created this eternal enemy, Amalek, ourselves. They tell us in *Sanhedrin* 99b that Amalek's forebearer wanted to convert to Judaism but was repulsed:

> Desiring to become a proselyte, she [Timna, see Genesis 36:22ff.] went to Abraham, Isaac, and Jacob, but they did not accept her. So she went and became a concubine to Eliphaz the son of Esau, saying, "I had rather be a servant to this people than a mistress of another nation." From her Amalek was descended who afflicted Israel. Why so? Because they should not have repulsed her.

Perhaps it is this ancient wrong that is righted at the end of the Book of Esther (8:17) when masses of people convert to, and find ready acceptance in, the Jewish faith and community.

Purim was apparently originally celebrated in Persia and Babylonia and eventually was adopted by the Jews of the Land of Israel. Purim was also called Mordecai Day. In 2 Maccabees 15:37, the holiday Nicanor Day, a celebration of a Maccabean victory over the Syrians, is described as falling on "the thirteenth of the twelfth month, called *Adar* in Aramaic, the day before Mordecai's Day." Purim falls on the fourteenth of the month of *Adar.* Both Nicanor Day and Mordecai Day celebrate the victory of Jews over tyrants, but the former celebrates a military victory and the latter a political and theological one. It is significant that the holiday that survived is the one that celebrates a religious triumph.

However, Hanukkah celebrates a military victory, does it not? Indeed, it did originally. But the account of that military victory, the two Books of the Maccabees, was not included in the Jewish Bible, and an alternative religious explanation for the festival of lights was provided by the rabbis in the tractate *Shabbat* 21b. Traditionally, this omission of the Books of the Maccabees is explained by the late date of Hanukkah (165 B.C.E.), after the Men of the Great Assembly had already set the canon of the *Tanach*. Others theorize that the rabbis consciously chose to emphasize Purim, the holiday that celebrates victory through faith and accommodation, over Hanukkah, which celebrates victory through military confrontation. The Book of Esther, which retells the former kind of victory, is not only included in the *Tanach* but has an entire tractate of the Talmud devoted to it, while the holiday that celebrates a military victory (Hanukkah) is covered in a few pages of *Gemara* (*Shabbat* 21a, ff.) and the books related to it were not included in the *Tanach*.

An objection may be raised to the designation of Purim as a book emphasizing religious triumph, because neither the name of God nor attention to strict religious observance are featured in this book. (Some commentators do see God's name in the first letters of the words of Esther 5:4, *yavo hamelech v'haman hayom, — yud hey vav hey—* and see a reference to God in 4:14, which states, "Relief and deliverance will rise for the Jews

from another place." The word "place," *makom*, is another
name for God. These words and letters are sometimes emphasized in the calligraphy of the *Megillah* itself.) However, just
because God is not explicitly mentioned does not make the
Book of Esther nonreligious in its outlook. On the contrary, the
book is carefully structured as a tale that reveals God as the
ultimate source of power and honor, the one entity that truly
controls the lives of the people in the story. No misdeed goes
unpunished, and obedience to God is rewarded.

Today we celebrate the holiday of Purim in four main
ways: we give gifts to the poor, read the *Megillah*, exchange
gifts (usually food, called *mishloach manot* or *shlach manos*), and
feast. These observances are suggested in the Book of Esther
itself (9:19–22):

> Therefore the Jews of the villages, who dwell in the unwalled
> towns, make the fourteenth day of the month Adar a day of
> gladness and feasting, and holiday, and of sending choice
> portions to one another. And Mordecai wrote these things, and
> sent letters to all the Jews who were in all the provinces of the
> king Ahashueros both near and far, to enjoin upon them that
> they should keep the fourteenth day of the month Adar, and the
> fifteenth day of the same, year by year, as the days on which the
> Jews rested from their enemies, and the month which was
> turned to them from sorrow to joy, and from mourning to
> holiday: that they should make them days of feasting and joy,
> and of sending choice portions to one another, and gifts to the
> poor.

In addition, we read from the Torah (Exodus 17:8–16), say the
blessing *Al HaNisim*, which thanks God for the miracles God
has performed for us, and we fast on the day preceding Purim.
Purim is also a day when the strict order of everyday life is
turned upside down. Usually we read Scriptures only in the
daytime, but on Purim the *Megillah* is read both in the evening
and in the morning. In addition, community leaders are poked
fun at during the Purim *shpiel* (a Purim satire).

Purim is quite precious among Jewish holidays. In his law
code, Maimonides (*Hilchot Moed, Megillah* 2:18) states that
Purim will even be celebrated in the World to Come:

In messianic times all the Prophetic Books and the Writings will cease to be used—except the Book of Esther. For this will continue to endure, just as the five books of the Law and the rules of the Oral Law will never be rescinded. And so, although all memory of ancient troubles will disappear, in accordance with the verse, "Because the former troubles are forgotten, and because they are hidden from mine eyes" (Isaiah 65:16), the days of Purim will not cease to be observed, as it is said, "And that these days of Purim should not fail from among the Jews, nor the memorial of them perish from their seed" (Esther 9:28).

\* \* \*

A few words on the style used in this book. Indented passages are selections from the Talmud or *Tanach*. The rest, so to speak, is commentary. Please note that the commentary accompanying any text may not reflect the conventional interpretation of that *sugyah*, that passage from the Talmud. Rather, it may be my extension or personal understanding of the passage. The selections of the *sugyot* are my own and are simply a sampling of the contents of each chapter. *Sugyot* are cited according to their traditional folio numbers. The front of each page in the Talmud is assigned a number and the letter a, the back of each page has that same number and the letter b.

The translations of the Talmud used in this book are adapted from the Soncino edition by Maurice Simon, first published in 1948. Although I have used gender-inclusive language in my commentary, translations of the language used to describe God in the Talmud are couched in the male gender.

# 1

## The Text

How does a relationship develop? It begins with the direct relationship of two people to each other. They learn what makes each other tick. They learn to bring out the best in each other. They even learn what troubles them about the other. When their relationship has progressed to a certain depth and maturity, they may consecrate their connection with a wedding ceremony: a ritual celebration of their relationship. As a married couple, they become part of a community and citizens of the world, together.

This progression describes not only the development of a relationship between two people, but also between a person and a holy text. First, we directly encounter the text. Then we consecrate such encounters by reading the text in a ritual context, such as on Shabbat mornings. Then the text we have taken into ourselves affects our relationship to our Jewish community and then to the world at large. This tractate outlines this progression of four stages in its four chapters. We begin with the foundation of the relationship: our direct, intense encounters with text.

**MISHNAH (2a):** The *Megillah* is read on the eleventh, the twelfth, the thirteenth, the fourteenth and the fifteenth [of *Adar*], neither earlier nor later. Cities which have been walled since the days of Joshua son of Nun read [the *Megillah* on the fifteenth (of *Adar*)]. Villages and big cities read [the *Megillah* on

3

the fourteenth (of *Adar*)]. However, the villages may push [the reading] forward to the day of meeting [i.e., Monday].

How [does this work out]? If the fourteenth [of *Adar*] fell on Monday, the villages and large towns read on that day and the walled places on the next day.

If it fell on Tuesday or on Wednesday, the villages push the reading forward to the Court Day [Monday], the large towns read on the day itself, and the walled places on the next day.

If [the fourteenth] fell on Thursday, the villages and large towns read on that day and the walled places on the next day.

If it fell on Friday, the villages push the reading forward to the Court Day and the large towns and walled places read on the day itself.

If it fell on Shabbat, the villages and large towns push the reading forward to the Court Day [Thursday], and the walled places read on the next day.

If it falls on Sunday, the villages push the reading forward to the Court Day [Thursday], and the large towns read on the day itself, and the walled cities on the day following.

Before we analyze the deeper message of this first *mishnah*, and the comments on it in the *gemara*, let us first examine its plain meaning. The following calendars summarize the material of the *mishnah*.

The system the rabbis use to regulate the reading of the *Megillah* is sensitive to two dimensions: time and the kind of community the reader comes from. The *mishnah* begins with the most basic case: People living in an unwalled city read the *Megillah* on its designated day, the fourteenth of *Adar*. If one lives in a small community that congregates only on the Court Days, which also served as the market days, then one may change the date of the reading so that it will fall on a day when the community congregates in any case. People living in walled cities celebrate the holiday on the fifteenth of *Adar*. This practice has its origin in the *Megillah*. We read there (9:17–19) that while the Jews in the provinces of Persia defeated their enemies, then rested on the fourteenth day of *Adar* (Purim Day for most of us), those in Shushan, a walled city, did not rest and feast until the fifteenth. In memory of the battle that was only won on the fifteenth of *Adar*, those who live in walled

| Monday | Tuesday | Wednesday | Thursday | Friday | Saturday | Sunday |
|---|---|---|---|---|---|---|
| 14 Villages, Towns | 15 Walled Cities | 16 | 17 | 18 | 19 | 20 |
| 13 Villages | 14 Towns | 15 Walled Cities | 16 | 17 | 18 | 19 |
| 12 Villages | 13 | 14 Towns | 15 Walled Cities | 16 | 17 | 18 |
| 11 | 12 | 13 | 14 Villages, Towns | 15 Walled Cities | 16 | 17 |
| 10 | 11 | 12 | 13 Villages | 14 Towns Walled Cities | 15 | 16 |
| 9 | 10 | 11 | 12 Villages, Towns | 13 | 14 | 15 Walled Cities |
| 8 | 9 | 10 | 11 Villages | 12 | 13 | 14 Towns |
| 15 Walled Cities | | | | | | |

cities celebrate the holiday on this later date. To this day, the *Megillah* is read in Jerusalem, a walled city, on the fifteenth of *Adar* rather than on the fourteenth. Tractate *Arachin* 32a lists examples of cities that have been walled since the days of Joshua ben Nun such as the old Castle of Sepphoris in the lower Galillee, the Fort of Gush-Halav (in the Galilee), Old Yotpat, Gamala (on the eastern shore of Lake Galilee), Gadud (perhaps Gadara or Gadar, east of the Jordan), Hadid (mentioned in Ezra 2:33, east of Lydda), Ono (modern Kefir Anneh, north of Lydda), Jerusalem, and the like.

The list of possible dates for the reading of the *Megillah* given in our *mishnah* shows with what flexibility the Megillah reading was treated. This degree of flexibility would be unthinkable regarding Shabbat or the Festivals. This may reflect Purim's relatively late development in the Jewish tradition or the low level of sanctity it is accorded in comparison with those more holy days. Clearly, keeping Shabbat takes precedence over reading the *Megillah*. We do not read the *Megillah* on Shabbat lest we carry it, an action forbidden on the Sabbath.

The rabbis here play on our expectations that they will begin this tractate, as they begin so many others, by defining the holiday in terms of its place in time. They begin with the question of Purim's time, only to show us that they will not focus on this aspect of the holiday in this tractate. Instead of defining the precise day of Purim, they tell us that the reading of the *Megillah* can take place on any one of *five* days. In other words, time is not a major determining factor in the subject they are truly discussing in this tractate: our relationship with the text. The core *mitzvah* of the holiday, reading the *Megillah* and, by extension, encounters with all our holy texts, will become the focus for the rabbis, rather than the time when we do so. This priority is even hinted at in the first words of this mishnah—*Megillah nikreit,* "the Megillah is read"—a title that concentrates on the text rather than on the time when it is read, that is, the day of Purim.

There could be several reasons for this priority of text over time. First, the holiday of Purim developed relatively late in Jewish history and may be a combination of various celebrations that were held on differing dates at this season. Second, Purim is not a festival ordained in the Torah, as are Passover, Sukkot, Shavuot, Rosh Hashanah, and Yom Kippur. The restrictions that apply to these festivals, such as the prohibitions against working, using fire, or carrying items, do not apply on Purim because it is not a *chag,* a festival mentioned in the Torah. Third, reading a text (here, the *Megillah*) is the heart of this holiday to a greater extent than a text is the heart of any other holiday. Sukkot, Pesach, Shavuot, and the High Holidays all had their special ritual observances: building a *sukkah,* bringing the Passover sacrifice, bringing the first fruits, blowing the *shofar,* and the purification rituals of the Temple. Even Hanukkah is marked by the lighting of candles. But Purim's most distinguishing feature is the reading of a text on the day. It is true that we also observe the day by feasting, exchanging gifts, and giving *tsedakah* (charity), but these are three actions that we perform on other occasions as well. We

feast at weddings and circumcisions. We exchange gifts frequently, and we should likewise give *tsedakah* as frequently as
possible. It is the primacy of text on Purim that makes it the
ideal context in which to explore our relationship with text in
general. This relationship is one that is, by definition, not
bound by time.

The reading of the *Megillah,* like the reading of the Torah
in the synagogue, is an echo of the moment of revelation on
Mount Sinai. Just as it takes a switch and a light bulb to complete
a circuit and turn on a light, so does revelation not only depend
on God; it requires *our* presence as well. Therefore, we read the
*Megillah* and the Torah when people are there to hear it.

In the ancient world, people gathered in the towns on
Mondays and Thursdays to sell their wares, and on Shabbat,
when they were at leisure to congregate. On those three days
of the week, Torah was read, and is still read, to this day. Since
it would be a burden on villagers to make an extra trip into
town in order to read the *Megillah* on a day when they did not
regularly congregate, they were permitted to read it on the
market days. However, those who lived in towns and walled
cities could easily reach the synagogue on any day, and it
would not have been a burden to travel to it on the exact day of
Purim (the fourteenth or fifteenth). Therefore, in those places
the *Megillah* was read on the proper day.

The origin of the practice of reading Torah on Mondays
and Thursdays seems unclear. The *gemara* attributes it to Ezra
the Scribe, who helped reestablish the Jewish practice of the
community in Israel when they returned from their exile in
Babylon in approximately 450–460 B.C.E. This origin would give
the custom great antiquity and authority. However, the rabbis
(in *Baba Kamma* 82a) link it to an even more ancient and
authoritative source: the forty-year period when the Israelites
wandered in the desert.

> The [following] ten enactments were ordained by Ezra: That
> the law be read [publicly] in the *Minchah* service on Sabbath;
> that the law be read [publicly] on Mondays and Thursdays; that
> Courts be held on Mondays and Thursdays . . .

"That the law be read [publicly] on Mondays and Thursdays."
But was this ordained by Ezra? Was this not ordained even before
him? For it was taught: "And they went three days in the wilderness and found no water" (Exodus 15:22), upon which those
who expound verses metaphorically said: Water means nothing
but Torah as it says, "Ho, everyone that thirsts come ye for water"
(Isaiah 55:1). It thus means that as they went three days without
Torah they immediately became exhausted. The prophets among
them thereupon rose and enacted that they should publicly read
the law on Sabbath, make a break on Sunday, read again on
Monday, make a break again on Tuesday and Wednesday, read
again on Thursday and then make a break on Friday so that they
should not be kept three days without Torah. . . .
"That Courts be held on Mondays and Thursdays"—when
people are about, as they come to read the Scroll of the Law.

In this _sugyah_ we see the tendency of the rabbis to link the
Jewish practices of their day to other ancient eras of Jewish
history, especially emphasizing the period when the Israelites
wandered in the wilderness. Here they link their tradition of
reading Torah three times a week to that time in the desert
when the Israelites wandered for three days without water. It
seems to be an accepted convention that water can refer to
Torah. The rabbis believed that Torah was as necessary as
water for the sustaining of life. Therefore, just as no one should
go three days without drinking water, the prophets ordained
that no one should go three days without reading Torah.

Perhaps the most significant part of this passage is the last
sentence. The rabbis of the Talmud subtly demonstrate their
system of priorities, for they attribute people's presence in
town on the market days not to their need to do business or
have disputes settled in court. These are secondary. They come
primarily to hear the Torah read, and all the economic and
social functions of the market day are based on this, not the
other way around. Torah is considered the basis of the community, not commerce or the legal system.

The rabbis' linkage of modern practice to ancient sources
can be seen in their commentary to our first _mishnah_. They do
not even comment on the date of Purim, at first. Rather, they
get to the heart of the true issue of the tractate: the nature of

revelation as it has been passed down through the generations. The *gemara* immediately traces the *Megillah* and Purim back through the chain of tradition to the source of rabbinic authority: the biblical text and their interpretation of it.

> **GEMARA (2a):** "The *Megillah* is read on the eleventh." Whence is this derived? . . . All these dates were laid down by the Men of the Great Assembly. For if you should think that the Men of the Great Assembly laid down only the fourteenth and fifteenth, [is it possible that] the [later] rabbis should have come and annulled a regulation made by the Men of the Great Assembly?! [It is not possible] for we have learnt, "One *Beit Din* (Jewish Court) cannot annul the ordinances of another unless it is greater to it in number and in wisdom"? Rather, it is obvious: all these days must have been laid down by the Men of the Great Assembly. Where are they hinted at [in the Scripture]? Rav Shemen bar Abba replied in the name of Rabbi Johanan, "Scriptures says, 'To confirm these days of Purim in their *times*' (Esther 9:31) [which indicates that] they laid down many 'times' for them."

The rabbis immediately attribute the practices of Purim to the Men of the Great Assembly, the legislative body that governed the Jewish people from approximately 500–200 B.C.E., several hundred years before the rabbis' time. This ancient body apparently met intermittently and left very few written records of its activities. The Men of the Great Assembly may, in fact, have set the practices of Purim, since they were forming many Jewish practices during this period. (It should be noted that there are those who believe that this body never existed at all.)

However, it may also be that the rabbis, or the Jewish public, established these practices at a later date and then wanted to lend these practices more authority by attributing them to an earlier generation. The acceptance of the holiday of Purim by the rabbis and the canonization of the *Megillah* were innovations in a tradition that venerated the ancient. Through the process of developing legends that gave new practices ancient roots, the rabbis could allow for both change *and* continuity with the past. These innovations were not innovations at all, rather, revivals of ancient practices.

Using the midrashic process, they immediately find a basis for the various dates of Purim in Scriptures. The *Megillah* states that the days of Purim are confirmed "in their *times*" (Esther 9:31). Since the word *times* is plural, it suggests that there are several times for the observance of this day. With this commentary on the mishnah, we see the difference between the *Mishnah*'s agenda and the *Gemara*'s. The *Mishnah* concentrates on Purim. The *Gemara* concentrates on the chain of tradition that brought us the text that we focus upon. The rabbis who composed the *Gemara* may concentrate on the chain of tradition here because they may have felt that this first mishnah was rather strange. They may have felt compelled to explain this *mishnah*'s existence, reassuring themselves, and the reader, that the material in this *mishnah* was authentic and authoritative, even though it differs so strongly from what we would have expected: a straightforward explanation of when Purim is celebrated. We can think of it in the following modern terms. Let us say that your family celebrates all the American holidays when everyone else does, except for Thanksgiving. Your family has its Thanksgiving turkey on the Friday night of Thanksgiving weekend. You would probably want an explanation of this strange custom in your normally traditional family. You might ask your mother about it, and she would then explain that the origin of this family custom goes back to her parents' generation, *and* their parents, and all the way back to your great-great-great grandparents. That is something like what the *Gemara* is doing here. They are tracing the origins of an anomalous practice (reading the *Megillah* on various dates) to an ancient and reliable source. This leads the *Gemara* to jump right into the heart of the tractate: the nature of revelation as it has been passed down through the generations in a reliable chain of tradition, and the impact of that revelation on our lives.

The *Gemara* traces the reading of the *Megillah* and Purim back through the chain of tradition to the source of rabbinic authority: the biblical text and their interpretation of it (their *drash* on Esther 9:31). They immediately attribute the practices of Purim to the Men of the Great Assembly. Traditional authorities believe that this body set the canon of the *Tanach*.

Since Esther is, even according to traditional thinkers, a late addition to the Scriptures, the Men of the Great Assembly are the most ancient source the *Megillah* reading could be traced back to.

The acceptance of the holiday of Purim by the rabbis, and the canonization of the *Megillah*, were innovations in a tradition that venerated the ancient. The rabbis saw these as innovations, surely. But they also saw them as consistent with ancient Jewish practices, and even saw them as revivals of ancient practices. The following *sugyah* explicitly deals with this tension between innovation and tradition and the way the rabbis resolved it.

> **GEMARA (2b):** Rabbi Jeremiah—or you may also say Rabbi Hiyya bar Abba—also said: [The final forms of the letters] *mem* (ם), *nun* (ן), *tsadi* (ץ), *pey* (ף), *caf* (ך), were prescribed by the Prophets. Do you really think so? Is it not written, "These are the commandments" (Leviticus 27:34), [which implies] that no prophet is permitted to introduce anything new henceforward? And further, Rav Hisda has said, "The mem (ם) and the samekh (ס) in the tablets (3a) remained [in place] by a miracle." That is so. They were in use, but people did not know which form came in the middle of a word and which one at the end of a word, and the Prophets came and ordained that the open forms should be in the middle of a word and the closed forms at the end of a word.
>
> Finally, [we still have the text] "these are the commandments," which [implies] that no prophet would ever introduce an innovation henceforward? Rather [say] that they were forgotten and the Prophets established them again.

Let us first examine the simple meaning of this *sugyah*. Here, the rabbis wonder how the final forms of the letters *caf, mem, nun, pey,* and *tsadi* came into existence. They also try to elucidate how it was decided that what we know as the final forms of the letters were fixed as the final forms. In other words, if you were looking at the Hebrew alphabet for the first time and no one told you which of the two forms of *caf* (ך,כ) is placed at the beginning and middle of words and which form is placed only at the end of words, you couldn't determine the order from just looking at the two forms of the letters.

Rabbi Jeremiah (or Hiyya bar Abba) suggests that it was the prophets who brought the final forms of the letters into being. However, an objection to this concept is immediately raised by those who believe the final forms of the letters have existed since the revelation at Sinai. The rabbis "prove" that the final letters have existed since Moses' day in two ways. First, they bring a proof text, the last sentence of the Book of Leviticus, which states, "These are the commandments which the Lord commanded Moses for the children of Israel in Mount Sinai" (Leviticus 27:34). The rabbis take this verse to mean that what was revealed at Mount Sinai may not be changed by later prophets, and a change in the alphabet in which these words were written on Mount Sinai would definitely be a change.

Next, Rav Hisda brings another "proof" that the final forms of the letters existed from the time of the revelation on Mount Sinai. According to the rabbis, the Tablets of the Law were written on both sides—carved all the way through. This being so, there was no physical way the insides of the final *mem* and the *samech* (ם,ס), which look almost like donuts, could be held in place. Therefore, the rabbis attribute their staying in place to a miracle. The main point of this story *here* is to show that the final form of the *mem,* and one assumes, the other letters with final forms, were in use from the days of Mount Sinai.

But if the final forms of the letters existed from the time of Mount Sinai, did the prophets play no role at all in the development of the final forms of these letters? This is the answer to the rabbis' second question: it is the prophets who decided that what we know as the final forms would actually be the final forms of the letters. But why did the prophets have to set this practice, if the final forms of the letters were already in use on Mount Sinai? Because, say the rabbis, at one time the people knew which were the final forms, but then they forgot them, and so the prophets had to "reset" this practice. This role of the prophets is even hinted at in the order in which these letters are cited in our *sugyah.* If the letters had been listed in alphabetical order, the text would have listed them as *caf, mem, nun, pey, tsadi.* However, the order presented—*mem, nun, tsadi, pey, caf*—plays on the words *min tsofim* (מן צופים), "from the-Watchmen," that is, the prophets.

What is going on in this *sugyah* on a deeper level? The rabbis are again showing the reliability of the chain of tradition—even when some links in that chain are weak. Even when parts of the tradition are forgotten by some or most of the Jewish people, the knowledge is preserved somewhere within the Jewish people and can be revived and made popular again in a later generation. If you think about the development of family stories, you can see this same process of forgetting and remembering at work. For example, many Jews who came to America were anxious to become Americans and tried to abandon the ways of the "old country" as quickly as possible. Their children, often embarrassed by their immigrant parents, tried to do the same. But many in the third generation were drawn to their grandparents' roots and sought to retrieve the memories, stories, and practices that were all but forgotten by their parents. Thus practices that seemed to have died were revived by a later generation. The chain of tradition is sustained, even when some of its links are weak. We will see this pattern of forgetting and remembering again.

The Jerusalem Talmud passage that corresponds to our *sugyah* [Jerusalem Talmud, *Megillah* 1:9, 12b, P'nei Moshe ed.] also emphasizes the strength of the chain of tradition in the transmission of the alphabet. There, the story is told of children who were playing a game to help themselves learn the final forms of the letters. They made a pun on the name of each letter with a final form (*mem, nun, tsadi, pey,* and *caf*), each pun playing on this concept of the reliable tradition. For the letter *mem,* the two forms of the letter stand for the transmission from one command to another command (in Hebrew: *mima'amar l'ma'amar,* ממאמר למאמר). The two forms of the letter *nun* stand for transmission from one faithful one to another faithful one (in Hebrew: *mine'eman l'ne'eman,* מנאמן לנאמן). The two forms of the letter *tsadi* represent the transmission from righteous one to righteous one (in Hebrew: *mitsadik l'tsadik,* מצדיק לצדיק). The two forms of the letter *peh* stand for the transmission from one mouth to another mouth (in Hebrew: *mipeh l'peh,* מפה לפה). And the two forms of the letter *caf* reminded them of the transmission of the Torah from the palm of the hand of the Holy One, Blessed be He, to the palm of the hand of Moses (in Hebrew: *micaf shel HaKadosh Baruch Hu el caf Moshe,* מכף של הקב"ה אל כף משה). In other words, these letters hint at the continuous process of passing on the revelation received at Sinai, one commandment at a time, from one righteous, faithful person to another, through the generations. (Many other beautiful stories and methods to learn the Hebrew alphabet can be found in tractate *Shabbat,* 104a. The development of the Hebrew alphabet is, in itself, a complex and fascinating topic. For more information, see the article "Alphabet, Hebrew," in the *Encyclopaedia Judaica,* vol. 1, pp. 674–750, which contains many illustrations and photographs.)

Now we must ask ourselves, "Were there truly no innovations in Judaism?" Far from it. Throughout the generations, Jewish custom and practice have changed. It is when these innovations are consistent with tradition, when they forge a new link in the chain, that we know they will last. For example, if that third-generation American Jew we mentioned above was relating her family history to her child, which do you think would truly last, a story the woman made up or a true story recapturing the family's history? The full-bodied, genuine history, with all its ups and downs, would be more likely to be passed on to her own grandchildren. So it is for us as a community: When our innovations do not tap into the "family history" of the Jewish people, they stand less of a chance of lasting.

Innovations consistent with the chain of tradition (or in some cases, not consistent with it) can be seen today as new English translations of the Tanach are brought forth in each generation to include new historical and archaeological insights, as well as to respond to changes in the English language. The rabbis, however, were troubled by the process of translating a holy text so it could be more easily understood by the masses. They understood the need for a translation, but how could they sanction this step away from the Torah they believed was given word for word by God? They justified it in the same way they justified other innovations: by attributing to it divine origins.

> **GEMARA (3a):** Rabbi Jeremiah – and some say Rabbi Hiyya bar Abba – also said, "The *Targum* (translation into Aramaic) of the Pentateuch was composed by Onkelos the proselyte under the guidance of Rabbi Eleazar and Rabbi Joshua."
>
> The *Targum* of the Prophets was composed by Jonathan ben Uzziel under the guidance of Haggai, Zechariah, and Malachi. And the Land of Israel [thereupon] quaked over an area of four hundred parsangs by four hundred parsangs. And a *Bat Kol* [a Heavenly Voice] came forth and said, "Who is this that has revealed My secrets to humanity?" Jonathan ben Uzziel stood and said, "I am the one who has revealed Your secrets to humanity. It is revealed and known before You that I have not done this for my own honor nor for the honor of father's house, but for Your honor have I done it, that disagreement may not increase in Israel."
>
> He further sought to reveal a *Targum* of the Writings, but a *Bat Kol* went forth and said to him, "Enough!" What was the reason? Because the date of the Messiah is foretold in it . . .
>
> How was it that [the land] did not quake because of the [translation of the] Pentateuch, while it did quake because of [that of] the Prophets? The meaning of the Pentateuch is explained, but the meaning of the Prophets is in some things explained and in others not explained.

We might be surprised by many things in this *sugyah*. For example, why was the Torah translated by a proselyte with the rabbis' guidance while the Prophets were translated with the help of prophets themselves? After all, the Torah is the primary text of our faith. The answer given by Steinsaltz and others is that the Torah is, by and large, a straightforward text, whereas the Prophets are written in a more poetic and visionary style, and thus more difficult to translate correctly.

We face a similar problem today when we attempt translations of the prayer book. The straightforward passages, such as the *Shema* and the *Amidah*, can be easily and meaningfully translated. However, some of the poems, acrostics, and *piy-*

*yutim* (hymns) either lose a great deal of their beauty in the translation or the translator must stray far from the original text to capture the rhythm of the poem. When a holy text is at stake, this difference between a poetically written original and its translation can be crucial.

The rabbis had to reconcile an innovation, the translation of the Prophets into Aramaic, with their view of tradition. They did so in a way similar to their explanation of the development of the final forms of the letters. They trace the translations of the Prophets back to the prophets themselves. This is somewhat problematic, because Jonathan ben Uzziel could certainly not have been personally tutored by the prophets Haggai, Zechariah, or Malachi. These three were the last of the prophets and lived in the fifth century B.C.E., while Jonathan ben Uzziel lived during the first century B.C.E. and the first century C.E. However, the rabbis surely knew this bit of history. They may have meant that the translations Jonathan ben Uzziel wrote down, and the insights they contained, were handed down in a continuous chain of tradition from the prophets Haggai, Zechariah, and Malachi until Jonathan wrote them down. His translation is not merely the transformation of the text from Hebrew to Aramaic, but also contains extensive and insightful commentary.

Clearly, Jonathan ben Uzziel's translation of the Prophets caused quite an uproar (one interpretation of the earth quaking: it "shook up" the Jewish community). The text states that a *Bat Kol* objected to Jonathan doing any more translations. When the rabbis spoke of a *Bat Kol*, they may have meant a voice out of heaven. However, they may also have referred to another meaning of this phrase: popular opinion (see Glossary). Whether the uproar came in the form of a voice from heaven or in consternation from scholars or the public, Jonathan's translation of Scripture into Aramaic may indeed have brought to light hidden meanings in the text that some may have preferred remained hidden.

An example may illustrate what it was in Jonathan's translation that caused such an uproar. Jonathan's *Targum* (translation) of the following verse is mentioned in *Sanhedrin* 94b:

"Foreasmuch as this people refuses the waters of Shiloah that go softly, and rejoice in Rezin and Remaliah's son. Now therefore behold the Lord brings up upon them the waters of the river, strong and many, even the king of Assyria, and all his glory: and he shall come up over all his channels, and go over all his banks" (Isaiah 8:6–7).

Rabbi Joseph said: But for the *targum* of this verse I would not know its meaning: Because this people have wearied of the Davidic dynasty, which rules them with gentleness like the waters of Shiloah which flow tranquilly, and have set their desire upon Rezin and the son of Ramaliah.

On the surface, the verses from Isaiah seem to have something to do with rivers and the king of Assyria, but, as Rabbi Joseph notes, they are quite difficult to understand. Clearly, the targum of this verse reveals some political meanings that might have remained hidden in the poetry of the text. Sennacherib was the king of Assyria and Babylonia from 705–681 B.C.E. He conquered many countries and tried to take Jerusalem from King Hezekiah, but failed. Sennacherib interpreted the utterance of the prophet Isaiah, quoted above, as a mandate to conquer Jerusalem. The image of water overflowing its banks may relate to the way Sennacherib dealt with rebellious Babylonians. Because controlling these rebels cost him men and money, Sennacherib decided to solve his "Babylonian problem" by destroying Babylon and letting the Euphrates River flow over it. We can now see that Jonathan's *Targum* is far more than a simple translation: it is a commentary that uncovers the following hidden meanings in the text.

Waters of Shiloah        = Davidic dynasty
Rezin and Remaliah's sons = Sennacherib
the waters of the river   = Sennacherib's flooding of
                            Babylon and its rebels

The rabbis were concerned that a similar Aramaic translation/commentary of the Hagiographa, the Writings, would reveal things best left hidden. For example, the rabbis believed that the date of the Messiah's arrival is predicted in the Book of Daniel, and therefore the rabbis did not want the Hebrew portions of that book translated into Aramaic (much of Daniel is written in Aramaic). Interestingly, the language of our *sugyah* switches from Hebrew to Aramaic after the word *Enough!* This may indicate that this last phrase, giving the detailed explanation about the Book of Daniel, is a later addition to this *sugyah*.

If the rabbis were troubled by the Book of Daniel, what objections did they have to translating the other books of the Writings into Aramaic? (In fact, there were Aramaic translations of Esther and Job.) Perhaps the rabbis insisted that the books of the Writings be read in Hebrew because some of them may have been composed quite late, under the influence of Greek (i.e., secular) culture. If they were to be read in Aramaic or Greek, they might sound more like Greek wisdom literature or love poems than Holy Scriptures.

The issue of translations is not an academic one. Today, a large number of Jews cannot read Hebrew with enough understanding to comprehend the text of the Bible in the original Hebrew. Should the text be brought to them in their languages, or should it remain only in its pure form? The answer is yes and no. Translations are undeniably important. Without them, many Jews would know very little of the Bible. However, there are nuances of meaning to be found, and associations to be made, that can be encountered only within the Hebrew text.

Before we leave this *sugyah,* we should note that it contains foreshadowing in three respects. Later in this chapter, the rabbis will discuss translation of the biblical text into Greek. In Chapter 3, the rabbis will discuss which passages of the Torah are not to be translated in the public reading of Scriptures in the synagogue, and in Chapter 4 they will include more stories of earthquakes heralding God's presence in Babylonia. The placement of these *sugyot* in their respective chapters corresponds to those chapters' themes. The issues regarding simple translations, that is, direct encounter with the text, are in Chapter 1, where this theme is explored in many ways. In Chapter 3, translation in the synagogue will be explored, which fits in with that chapter's theme of the text in the Jewish community. In Chapter 4, the rabbis examine our encounters with God as we live in exile from the Land of Israel, which corresponds to the theme of that chapter: God's presence in the world at large.

These compositional touches are important clues that help us see this tractate as an integrated whole. (After all, if the rabbis simply wanted to group together all the *sugyot* dealing with translations of the *Tanach*, they could have put the *sugyah* from Chapter 3 here, in Chapter 1.) One could read this tractate as if it were composed of two unrelated sections: two chapters on the *Megillah*, followed by two unrelated chapters on the reading of Torah. Such a reading misses the core idea that unifies the tractate: the nature of the Tanach and its impact on various spheres of our lives.

Our next *sugyah* clearly shows us how important it is to show the proper honor to people and to our holy texts.

**GEMARA (3a):** And is the [Temple] Service more important than the study of Torah? . . . (3b) And Rav Shmuel bar Uniah said, "The study of Torah is greater than the daily sacrifices." . . . There is no contradiction. Here [in the latter case], the [study] of many [people is referred to]. And here [in the former case, the study] of an individual [is referred to].

Rava said, It is obvious to me that [between the Temple] service and the reading of the *Megillah*, the reading of the *Megillah* takes precedence . . .

[As between the] study of the Torah and the reading of the *Megillah*, the reading of the *Megillah* takes precedence . . .

[As between the] study of the Torah and attending to a *meit mitzvah* (a body which no one claims and buries and the burial of which is a religious duty), [attending to] a *meit mitzvah* takes precedence, since it has been taught: The study of the Torah may be neglected in order to perform the last rites or to bring a bride to the canopy.

[As between the] Temple service and attending a *meit mitzvah*, attending to a *meit mitzvah* takes precedence . . .

[As between the] reading of the *Megillah* and [attending to] a *meit mitzvah*, which takes precedence? Shall I say that the reading of the *Megillah* takes precedence in order to proclaim the miracle, or perhaps [the burying of] a *meit mitzvah* takes precedence because of the respect due to human beings? After propounding the question, he himself answered it saying, "[Burying] a *meit mitzvah* takes precedence, since a Master has said, "Great is the [obligation to pay due] respect to human beings, since it overrides a negative precept of the Torah."

This *sugyah* is a key one in understanding the rabbis' system of priorities regarding who, or what, deserves honor. We might summarize their discussion with the following continuum of honor:

1. *Meit Mitzvah* >
2. Reading *Megillah* >
3. Communal Torah Study >
4. Temple Service >
5. Torah study of an individual.

Judaism holds the honor of each human being quite dear. It is a profanation of God when a person, created in God's image, lies dead with no one to attend the corpse. Every person is entitled to the baseline level of respect of a decent burial, and Jewish law emphatically underlines this point. Even someone taking his son to be circumcised, a very great *mitzvah*, stops performing that *mitzvah* to attend to a *meit mitzvah* (see Halachic Appendix).

The reading of the *Megillah* ranks next in the rabbis' system of honor. The public proclamation of God's power, and the consequent reaffirmation of our relationship with God, may take precedence over Torah study for several reasons. The reading of the *Megillah* is a time-bound, positive commandment: it is something we must do at a certain time. Communal Torah study is a positive commandment, but it is not time bound: we may, and should, do it as frequently as possible. In addition, the reading of the *Megillah* involves the entire community. Torah study might not have involved everyone in as unifying a way as the reading of the *Megillah* does. The Temple cult involved fewer aspects of a person's life than did Torah study. The perpetual sacrifices were our way of communicating with God, but public Torah study, during which people learned how to behave twenty-four hours a day, affected more spheres of their lives. Finally, Torah study by an individual involves the fewest number of people and, consequently, the least communal affirmation of our relationship with God.

What are the key criteria the rabbis are using to determine their rank ordering of honor? First, all these activities enhance our relationship with God. Within that set of activities, those activities that bring honor to humanity, either through their intensity or the large number of people they involve, rank higher. The care of a *meit mitzvah* clearly ranks the highest: human dignity must be shown honor. After that, those activities that bring the greatest number of people in touch with God through text or practice take priority. The more people an activity involves in holiness, the greater honor is accorded that activity.

This rank-ordering system seems clear and logical when we think of it in the context of a modern synagogue. Imagine you are at Purim services, reading the *Megillah*, when someone rushes in and says there is an abandoned corpse on the lawn. You would naturally stop reading the *Megillah* and rush out to care for the corpse, call the police, and so forth. Imagine again that you were in a Torah study class when someone told you it was time for the *Megillah* reading. You would naturally stop studying and go hear the *Megillah* read (although if the class were quite wonderful, you might be tempted to keep studying). On the next level we might imagine that you had a choice between attending a daily worship service that had already achieved a *minyan* (our best modern equivalent to the Temple service) or hearing a lecture on Torah by a great sage. The rabbis deem it a greater *mitzvah* for you to attend the lecture by the sage than to attend the daily *minyan*. Finally, if you were sitting alone studying Torah and someone called you to participate in a worship service, it would be a greater *mitzvah* for you to participate in the service than to continue studying.

Holiness for the rabbis is a combination of *time, people,* and *text.* And so the rabbis mandate that the leaders teach the people about each holiday from the appropriate text in its season.

**GEMARA (4a):** If Purim falls on a Sabbath, we ask and expound on the subject of the day. Why mention Purim? The same rule applies to festivals also, as it has been taught: Moses ordained for Israel that they should ask and expound on the subject of the day—the laws of Passover on Passover, the laws of Shavuot on Shavuot, and the laws of Sukkot on Sukkot!

This *sugyah* is quite straightforward and needs little explanation. It is important because this *sugyah* will be mentioned again at the very end of this tractate, another small indication of how carefully this document is put together. If the rabbis' goal was merely to cite this piece of tradition, then they would not have to repeat it at the end of the tractate. However, this *sugyah* is used again at the end of our tractate to help sum up the volume's contents.

Given that time, text, and people are the building blocks of holiness, if one part of this formula is missing, another must be augmented. So, for example, when the text of the *Megillah* is not read in its exact time, we must augment the number of people who hear it, in order to create the proper holiness for this *mitzvah*.

> **GEMARA (5a):** Rav said, "On the actual day of Purim, the *Megillah* can be read even by an individual, but on the alternative days it should be read only in a company of ten."

Here the rabbis demonstrate a keen awareness of how important belonging to a unified religious community can be. Anyone who has celebrated a Jewish holiday in Israel (or Brooklyn) knows the tremendous feelings of affirmation and belonging that come from being able to look around and know that almost everyone is celebrating the holiday with you. Shabbat in Jerusalem is surely sweeter than anywhere else on earth: People walking to synagogue in the streets because there is no traffic; hearing Shabbat songs being sung as you walk past apartment buildings. When we do not have such a global affirmation of our observances of the *mitzvot*, we must create a community so we can feel it. Therefore, on the actual day of Purim, when everyone is reading the *Megillah*, we may read it by ourselves, alone, because we feel part of a larger community that is reading the *Megillah*. But if we do not read the *Megillah* on the day of Purim itself, then we need ten people to create that community feeling that is part of holiness.

Holiness and Torah in our lives lead us to a sense of reverence and honor for the wonders Torah brings us. The

*Gemara* now begins to deal with this issue of honor more directly. Who deserves honor, and how is it shown? This immediately brings out a thornier issue: Why do those who do *not* seem to deserve honor receive it?

**GEMARA (6b):** Rabbi Isaac also said: If a man says to you, "I have labored and not found," do not believe him. If he says, "I have not labored and have found," do not believe him. If he says, "I have labored and found," believe him. These words apply to words of Torah, but business depends on the help of heaven. And even for words of Torah this is true only of penetrating to the meaning, but for remembering what one has learnt, all depends on the assistance of heaven.

Rabbi Isaac also said: If you see a wicked man being favored by fortune, do not contend with him, as it is said, "Do not contend with evildoers" (Psalm 37:1).

Nor is this all, but he may even prosper in his undertakings, as it is said, "His ways prosper at all times" (Psalm 10:5).

Nor is this all, but he may even be judged right, as it is said, "Your judgments are far above out of his sight" (Psalm 10:5).

Nor is this all, but he may even triumph over his enemies, as it is said, "As for all his adversaries, he puffs at them" (Psalm 10:5).

Is this so? Has not Rabbi Johanan said in the name of Rabbi Simeon bar Yohai: It is permitted to contend with the wicked in this world, as it is said, "They that forsake the Torah praise the wicked, but such as keep the Torah contend with them" (Proverbs 28:4).

Also it has been taught: Rabbi Dosethai bar Matoon said: It is permitted to contend with the wicked in this world. And if one should whisper to you saying, [As for the text] "Do not contend with evildoers, neither be envious against them that work unrighteousness" (Psalm 37:1), one whose heart pounds (i.e., one who is afraid) speaks thus. . . .

Rav Huna said: What [is the meaning of] what is written, "Wherefore look you when they deal treacherously, and hold your peace when the wicked swallow up the man that is more righteous than he" (Habbakuk 1:13)? A person more righteous than himself, he can swallow up. A completely righteous person he cannot swallow up. If you like I can say that when fortune is smiling on him, the case is different.

Why does all of our work and our striving to be good sometimes appear not to avail us? The rabbis simply confirm that this is, indeed, a mystery. They seek to reassure the reader that at least in learning, effort surely brings reward. However, they know that for some people, learning and remembering come more easily than for others. They seem to recognize that different individuals may have different learning styles. A person might be quite perceptive and gifted without having the gift of memory that they prized so highly.

While the rabbis seem to accept that the wicked prosper, their acceptance goes only so far. We can also fight the wicked, as Esther did. After all, Haman appeared to succeed: He was the power behind the throne. Yet he was ultimately vanquished by the combined efforts of people and God. The rabbis may have chosen to make *drashot* continuously on Psalm 10 because it asks (and answers) the very question that concerns them. "Why do You stand far off O Lord? Why do you hide Yourself in times of trouble?" (Psalm 10:1).

In the end, what insight do the rabbis give us to help us cope with the evil person who is honored and the righteous person who is not honored? As usual, they give no pat answers for problems that have no readily evident solutions. There simply are times when the wicked flourish and the righteous suffer. Sometimes contending with evil avails us. Sometimes it is better to leave the situation alone. (These days, one is reminded of the advice that if someone with a gun comes to rob your store, you should make it the most efficient transaction of the day.) Esther struggled with just such a decision before she determined that she should intercede with Ahashueros on behalf of the Jews. She decided to contend with the wicked Haman, even though it might not avail her.

This is one of Judaism's strengths: it does not give us hopeful, absolute answers when they do not correspond to reality. By refusing to guarantee us that we will prosper if righteous and suffer if evil, the rabbis are urging us to do right for its own sake, not for the sake of honor or reward. In the end, this reflects a higher level of moral development, and one that has a better chance of enduring within individuals, for it depends on inner rewards, not external ones.

Honor, too, in the Jewish system, is based on internal values, not external ones. As we have already noted, at first glance Esther appears to be a secular book. However, when we look into it more carefully, we see that God is active throughout the story, though never named. It is this discrepancy between the external form and the internal spirit of the Book of Esther that may have caused some controversy regarding its inclusion in the *Tanach*.

> **GEMARA (7a):** Rav Samuel bar Judah said: Esther sent to the Wise Men saying, "Commemorate me for generations!" They sent back to her, "You will awaken the envy of the nations against us." She sent back to them, "I am already recorded in the chronicles of the kings of Media and Persia" (Esther 10:2). . . .
> Rav Judah said in the name of Samuel: [The scroll] of Esther does not make the hands unclean. Are we to infer from this that Samuel was of the opinion that Esther was not composed under the inspiration of the Holy Spirit? [How can this be, seeing that] Samuel has said that Esther was composed under the inspiration of the Holy Spirit? It was composed to be recited [by heart], but not to be written.

First, let us go through the simple meaning of this *sugyah*. Here, the *Gemara* portrays Esther herself as demanding that her story be canonized—included in the *Tanach*. The Wise Men (perhaps referring to the Men of the Great Assembly) seem uncomfortable with this idea, fearing that if they set down Esther's story in writing, it would awaken the wrath of the nations against the Jews. However, Esther, or those who favored the canonization of Esther, retort by quoting the Book of Esther itself, which says that "the full account of the greatness of Mordecai, how the king advanced him, are they not written in the book of the chronicles of the kings of Media and Persia?" (Esther 10:2). In other words, the story of Purim was already written down by the very nations the sages were worried about. Therefore there could be no further harm in canonizing the *Megillah* among the Jews. We can understand the sages' hesitation if we think of an analogous situation in American history. The forces led by Custer were badly beaten by Native Americans at the Battle of Little Big Horn. If the Native Americans were to celebrate the anniversary of this victory every year with a solemn reading of an account of the battle, even while their territory was occupied by white Americans, some Native Americans might feel this would tempt the whites to treat them harshly. Other Native Americans might feel that, since this battle was already well documented in the country's history, there would be no reason not to celebrate the day and compose an accepted ritual account of the events of Custer's Last Stand. This refutation seems to settle that objection, but then another is quickly raised.

There seems to be a dispute about whether the Scroll of Esther makes the hands unclean. In other words, is it one of those books that is protected—included in the canon? Samuel seems to think that the *Megillah* does not make the hands unclean, that is, is not included in the canon. This poses a problem, since Samuel himself has stated that the *Megillah* was composed under the influence of the Holy Spirit, so how could it possibly *not* be in the canon? The *Gemara* resolves this contradiction by stating that the *Megillah*, while composed under the inspiration of the Holy Spirit, was meant to be recited orally, not written down, and thus the physical scroll itself and the letters in it would not have the holiness that makes the hands unclean. Again, if we harken back to our Custer's Last Stand story, we might suppose that the Native Americans who wanted to celebrate this anniversary might discuss whether the story alone was to be standardized but could be written in any form—the paper having no special significance—or whether the actual paper itself on which the story was written was to be guarded and standardized. If they were like the rabbis, they would eventually decide that both the story and the paper on which it was written should be standardized and guarded.

The phrase "defiles the hands," which refers to a book that is holy, may seem puzzling at first. Why should a holy book defile the hands? There are several explanations for this practice. The Talmud tells us (*Shabbat* 14a):

And why did the rabbis impose uncleanness upon Scripture books? Rav Mesharshiya said, "Because originally *terumah* foods were stored near Torah scrolls, for they argued: This is holy and that is holy. When it was seen that the books came to harm, the rabbis imposed uncleanness upon them."

In the Temple in Jerusalem, the priests and Levites were entitled to eat *terumah*, part of the food tribute paid them as priests. This was an important "perk" for the priests and their families, who were also allowed to eat this *terumah*. Today, we might see executives in a company offered free meals at lunch and catered meals to take home from the company cafeteria as an analogous situation. However, let us imagine that one of these executives took her food and stored it next to some beautiful artwork she had in her office and that mice came and ate her food—and kept eating right into the artwork! The CEO might then set down a ruling: no more storing food next to valuable artwork. That is similar to our situation here. The priests would put their *terumah* food next to the Torah scrolls, and the mice would eat through the *terumah and* the scrolls. Since the priests could only eat the *terumah* when they were in a state of purity, by making the Torah scrolls unclean, the rabbis forced the priests to store the Torah scrolls in a safe place away from the *terumah*.

Of course, there are alternative explanations. Zeitlin (1933) saw in this designation the result of a fight between two groups of Jewish leaders who existed in the period before the destruction of the Second Temple: the Pharisees and the Sadducees. The Pharisees, the predecessors of the rabbis, believed that there were two Torahs: the Written one and the Oral one. They also believed in resurrection of the dead and tended to represent the interests of the middle and lower classes. The Sadducees, on the other hand, believed only in the Written Torah, not the Oral one, did not believe in the resurrection of the dead, and tended to represent the interests of the upper classes, including the priests who ministered in the Temple. These priests had to be in a state of ritual purity in order to perform their ritual duties in the Temple. If by touching a certain book a priest defiled his hands, then he could not perform his ritual functions. This ruling made studying the Oral Torah, rather than the Written Torah, more desirable for the priests and anyone else who strictly observed the laws of ritual purity, as the Sadducees did, because the Oral Torah did not defile their hands and disqualify them from priestly service—just the result that the Pharisees desired! This is a very brief summary of a complicated issue, and of course many people would disagree with Zeitlin's theories about Scriptures defiling the hands.

We must deal with one last issue regarding the defiling of the hands. When we think of ritual impurity, we may think of it in a negative sense. Quite the contrary: the more something is to be honored, the more impure the rabbis made it. Designating something as impure is a way of protecting it. *Mishnah Yadayim* 4:6 states: "The Holy Scriptures, their uncleanness corresponds to their preciousness." We can think of it in the following way. When shopping for jewelry, we can pick up rhinestones right off the counter. If we want cubic zirconia, we have to have them brought out of the cases. If we want diamonds, we must have them brought from a vault. The more precious something is, the more barriers there are between us and that object.

What qualifies a book for canonization in the Jewish Bible? Clearly, one of the criteria used to determine which books belonged to the canon was their inspiration from the Holy Spirit. There was no question that the Torah, the first five books of the Bible, or the stories and poems of the prophets, were divinely inspired. In fact, the Torah and the Prophets were composed while Israel still merited prophecy, direct communication from God. However, according to *Tosefta Sotah* 13:2 and *Yoma* 9b, after the prophets Haggai, Zechariah, and Malachi prophesied, "the Holy Spirit departed from Israel, but they still availed themselves of the *Bat Kol* (a Heavenly Voice)." The Book of Esther was composed after the time the Talmud states that prophecy ceased. Therefore its canonical status was not as clear to the rabbis as the books in the Torah and Prophets.

What is exalted about this book? It is holy because the Jewish people held it to be holy and divinely inspired. Some rabbis may not have wanted to include it in the canon, but the people demanded its inclusion in the *Tanach*. That is one interpretation of the paragraph that begins this *sugyah*. The cry they attribute to Esther might actually have been a popular outcry for the canonization of the *Megillah*.

Theories about the method and date of the canonization of the Book of Esther obviously vary widely. What does seem clear is that the Jewish people wanted the Book of Esther to be included in the Jewish Bible and that they found the holiday of Purim and the story of Esther meaningful. Some scholars theorize that the holiday of Purim actually predates the Book of Esther. By this reckoning, the Book of Esther may have served to raise the religious status and meaning of the holiday.

The rabbis have frequently had to canonize, or include as normative, materials or practices to which they objected. For example, the rabbis tried for centuries to expunge the recitation of *Kol Nidre* from the Yom Kippur service, but never succeeded because it was popular with the people. In Judaism, definitions of normative practice rise up from the people; they are rarely imposed down upon them.

Wise leaders have been guided by the Jewish people from its very earliest days. For example, when Hillel came to the Land of Israel from Babylon, he was appointed *Nasi*, or president, because of his sound reasoning *and* because he listened to the people, as the following story from *Pesachim* 66a illustrates.

[When Hillel came from Babylonia to the Land of Israel] they immediately set him at their head and appointed him *Nasi* over them, and he was sitting and lecturing the whole day on the laws of Passover.

He began rebuking them with words. Said he to them, "What caused it for you that I should come up from Babylonia to be *Nasi* over you? It was your indolence, because you did not serve the two greatest men of the time, Shemaya and Avtalion."

Said they to him, "Master, what if a man forgot and did not bring a knife [to slaughter the Passover lamb] on the eve of the Sabbath?"

"I have heard this law," he answered, "but have forgotten it. But leave it to Israel: if they are not prophets, yet they are the children of prophets!" On the morrow, he whose Passover was a lamb stuck it [the knife] in its wool. He whose Passover was a goat stuck it between its horns. He saw the incident and recollected the *halachah* and said, "Thus have I received the tradition from the mouth[s] of Shemaya and Avtalion."

First, let us examine the simple meaning of this story. We can almost picture Hillel arriving in the Land of Israel and immediately beginning to teach the people the laws of Passover. He must have been dismayed that they had forgotten these laws so thoroughly, especially since they had had the opportunity to study with two of the greatest Jewish teachers of any age, Shemaya and Avtalion. It is no wonder that he rebuked the people for learning from him what they could have learned from these two great teachers.

The people then wanted to know what a person should do in the following circumstance. When the first evening of Passover fell on Shabbat, and a person was preparing to bring his Passover lamb to the Temple to be slaughtered, he was supposed to bring his knife, with which to slaughter the lamb, to the Temple before evening fell, so that he would not carry it on Shabbat. If he forgot to make these preparations, how was he to convey the knife to the Temple without violating the Shabbat? By lodging it in the wool or between the horns of the sacrificial animal, he could accomplish his task without violating Shabbat. However, Hillel could not remember this law, nor could he reason it out from the text. Only when Hillel saw the people doing this could he decree what the law was.

There is symmetry in this story. We have here two examples of the forgetting of traditions and their reinstitution, just as we saw in our second *sugyah* on page 2b. In the first case of forgetting, Hillel sternly rebukes the public. In the second instance of forgetting, Hillel's own, more mercy is shown. When Hillel forgot a law, the people of Israel did not rebuke him, even though he was a teacher of the Oral Torah and was charged to remember. Only when Hillel was shown how to behave charitably by the people, did he remember to show the people the honor due them. He then looked to them for guidance on Jewish practice when he could not remember the law. This story demonstrates the role of the people in Judaism as the repository of God's spirit and knowledge. (This story has also been interpreted as a subtle reminder that while we may creatively interpret texts in order to determine Jewish practice, we must rely on our ancient traditions to guide us, as well.) As with the canonization of Esther, the inclusion of *Kol Nidre* in the

Yom Kippur liturgy, and other practices, the people are the ultimate arbiters of Jewish practice when they remember, in word and deed, their ancient teachings.

In the next *sugyah*, the rabbis demonstrate another method by which to encounter and understand the text: the level of *remez* (hints in the text), here demonstrated through *Gematria*.

> **GEMARA (7b):** Raba said: It is the duty of a man to mellow himself [with wine] on Purim until he cannot tell [the difference] between "cursed be Haman" and "blessed be Mordecai."

How does one rejoice? The rabbis tell us that women are gladdened by new clothes and men are gladdened by wine (*Pesachim* 109a). In fact, the *halachah* states that women receive a new outfit of clothes for each of the three pilgrimage festivals, and men receive wine. Men are required to drink the four cups of wine at the Passover *seder* and make *kiddush* on the other festivals and on Shabbat. However, only on Purim and Simchat Torah did it become a tradition to drink to excess.

A man was to become so intoxicated that he could not tell the difference between the hero and villain in the story. This injunction may have helped people relax and rejoice in the holiday. However, today substance abuse, including alcoholism, is a serious problem in the Jewish community. Perhaps we need to rethink how we celebrate this holiday and abstain from excessive drinking on it.

The two phrases cited in this *sugyah*, "Cursed is Haman" (in Hebrew: *Arur Haman*) and "Blessed is Mordecai" (in Hebrew: *Baruch Mordecai*) have the same numerical value in *Gematria*, the system that attributes a numerical value to each Hebrew letter. So,

| | |
|---|---|
| *Arur Haman* (ארור המן) | = |
| *aleph* (א) | = 1 |
| *reish* (ר) | = 200 |
| *vav* (ו) | = 6 |
| *reish* (ר) | = 200 |
| *hey* (ה) | = 5 |
| *mem* (מ) | = 40 |
| *nun* (נ) | = 50 |
| | 502 |

| | |
|---|---|
| and *Baruch Mordecai* (ברוך מרדכי) | = |
| *bet* (ב) | = 2 |
| *reish* (ר) | = 200 |
| *vav* (ו) | = 6 |
| *caf* (כ) | = 20 |
| *mem* (מ) | = 40 |
| *reish* (ר) | = 200 |
| *dalet* (ד) | = 4 |
| *caf* (כ) | = 20 |
| *yud* (י) | = 10 |
| | 502 |

What hidden meaning could be hinted at in the equivalence of these two phrases? Is it that blessing Mordecai and cursing Haman are equally good deeds? Or is it that the blessing of Mordecai by Ahashueros led to the cursing of Haman? Or that the blessing bestowed on Mordecai felt like a curse to Haman? Is a wicked person as pained when the righteous are blessed as the righteous are pained when the wicked are blessed? This equivalence may hint at an even more hidden level of meaning: the external blessings and curses of this world are equivalent and therefore not as full of meaning as we often assume them to be. There is another level of blessings and curses that may be more significant than the ones we see on the surface in this world.

We have in this tractate a long series of *mishnayot* that all begin with the phrase "There is no difference between. . . ." For example, the first *mishnah* in this series states,

**Mishnah (7b):** There is no difference between festivals and Sabbath save only in the matter of [preparing] food.

What is noteworthy about this series of similar *mishnayot* is how the *Gemara* comments at length only on those *mishnayot* that touch on the subjects they wish to address, that is, the studying of text and the honor due us when we engage in this activity. Often we assume that the *Mishnah* gives shape to the *Gemara,* and this is, of course, true. However, the *Gemara* also shapes the way the *Mishnah* is used and interpreted and selects which *mishnayot* to emphasize by commenting on some *mish-*

*nayot* more extensively than on others. This phenomenon is so notable in this chapter that it can be seen just by glancing through these pages of the tractate (7b–17a) and noting how much *Gemara* commentary is attached to each *mishnah*. Only the last two *mishnayot* in the series, which deal with revelation and honor, the topics the *Gemara* wishes to emphasize, are commented on at length. The following *mishnah*, which describes different kinds of holy texts, gives the rabbis the perfect "jumping off point" from which to explore this theme.

> **MISHNAH (8b):** There is no difference between books [of the Scripture] and *tefillin* and *mezuzot* save that the books may be written in any language whereas the *tefillin* and *mezuzot* may be written only in Assyrian [script of Hebrew]. Rabban Simeon ben Gamaliel says that books [of the Scripture] also were permitted [by the sages] to be written only in Greek.

First we must examine the basic differences between the Tanach and the short selections from it that we find in *tefillin* and *mezuzot*. *Mezuzot*, which contain two passages from the Torah, Deuteronomy 6:4–9 and Deuteronomy 11:13–21, are attached to the doorposts of our houses. *Tefillin* consist of small boxes containing the Torah passages Exodus 13:1–10, Exodus 13:11–16, Deuteronomy 6:4–9, and Deuteronomy 11:13–21, which are bound to the head and arm. When contained in the *mezuzah* and *tefillin*, the Torah texts cited above are signs of our committed relationship with God, and as such, have a different status from these same passages when they are simply read from the Torah. It can be likened to the difference between a diamond ring that is worn as an engagement ring and that same diamond ring when it is worn as a cocktail ring. It is beautiful in both cases, but in the former case, it has added significance. And just as a diamond ring must be worn only on the ring finger of the left hand in order to have that significance, so the texts of the *mezuzah* and *tefillin* must contain *exactly* the words prescribed in the Torah, if they are to have their added meaning. Thus the Torah texts in *tefillin* and *mezuzot* must be written in Hebrew, in the accepted Hebrew script.

Does the same apply to the words of Torah that we read? Are these words just as filled with holiness when we read them in translation as they are when we read them in the Hebrew? Rabban Simon ben Gamaliel gives a relatively lenient ruling, permitting Torah scrolls to be written in Greek as well as in Hebrew. (Greek was the language used throughout the ancient world.) It would be analogous to writing a Torah scroll in English today and proclaiming it to be as holy as a Torah scroll written in Hebrew. In fact, the law still permits us to write a Torah scroll in Greek; however, it has become the custom not to do so.

This dilemma that Rabban Gamaliel faced—the tension between reading holy texts in the original or in translations that everyone can understand—is a problem faced throughout Jewish history, as our *Gemara* now shows. The rabbis comment on the effect of translation of the Torah, using the Greek translation of the Bible, known as the Septuagint, as their prime example.

**GEMARA (9a):** Our rabbis permitted them [Scrolls of the Scripture] to be written only in Greek. And it is taught, Rabbi Judah said: Even when our rabbis permitted Greek, they permitted it only for a scroll of the Torah.

This was on account of the incident [related in connection with] King Ptolemy, as it has been taught: It is related of King Ptolemy that he brought together seventy-two elders and placed them in seventy-two houses, without telling them why he had brought them together, and he went in to each one of them and said to them, "Translate for me the Torah of Moses your master." God then gave into the heart of each one of them counsel and they all agreed on the same idea and wrote for him,

[1] "God created in the beginning" (Genesis 1:1).

[2] "I shall make man in image and likeness" (Genesis 1:26).

[3] "And He finished on the sixth day, and rested on the seventh day" (Genesis 2:2).

[4] "Male and female He created him" (Genesis 5:2), and they did not write "created them."

[5] "Come let me descend and confound their tongues" (Genesis 11:7).

[6] "And Sarah laughed among her relatives" (Genesis 18:12).

[7] "For in their anger they slew an ox and in their wrath they dug up a stall" (Genesis 49:6).

[8] "And Moses took his wife and his children and made them ride on a carrier of men" (Exodus 4:20).

[9] "Now the time that the children of Israel dwelt in Egypt and in other lands was four hundred years" (Exodus 12:40),

[10] "And he sent the elect of the children of Israel" (Exodus 24:5).

[11] "And against the elect of the children of Israel he put not forth his hand" (Exodus 24:11) (9b).

[12] "I have taken not one valuable of theirs" (Numbers 16:15);

[13] "Which the Lord your God distributed to give light to all the peoples" (Deuteronomy 4:19);

[14] "And he went and served other gods which I commanded should not be served" (Deuteronomy 17:3).

According to this text and another called the Letter of Aristeas, King Ptolemy Philadelphus of Egypt (285–247 B.C.E.) commissioned a translation of the Torah into Greek, which is known as the Septuagint. According to the letter, the king brought seventy-two elders from the Land of Israel to Egypt, and there feted them for ten days while he listened to their wisdom. Then he sent them to an island where they produced a translation of the Torah in seventy-two days. The Alexandrian Jewish community, which tended to be assimilated yet Jewishly observant, accepted and used this translation. There is one traditional view that holds this translation of the Torah into Greek as an unfortunate occurrence. According to this view, Ptolemy was an evil king who forced these seventy-two men to write this translation by locking them into rooms. It was only then that God intervened and caused each of them to write the exact same translation of the text.

This *sugyah* clearly reveals much about what in the Torah the rabbis had difficulty explaining to others. It is almost as if they were saying, "If we only had a chance to rewrite the Torah, we would change the following phrases, so that we would not have to explain them, as we have been forced to do." Let us look at each verse in turn to see what troubled the rabbis.

1. **Genesis 1:1 states,** "In the beginning God created" *(Bereishit bara Elohim)*. The Greek translation of this verse reads, "*God* created in the beginning," with God's name first. This translation solves the following problem: some Gnostics (those who believe in two gods), reading this verse, claimed that there were two forces who created the world—a force called *Bereishit* and God. The reversal in word order would nullify their ability to make that claim, since it would clearly make God the sole subject of the sentence.

2. **Genesis 1:26 says,** "Let *us* make Man in *our* image, after *our* likeness." The use of the words "us" and "our" again plays into the Gnostic idea of two gods instead of just one. The translation "*I* shall make man in image and likeness" solves this problem.

3. **Genesis 2:2 says,** "And God finished on the seventh day His work which He had made," which might be interpreted to mean that God did some work on Shabbat. Therefore the translation "And He finished on the sixth day, and rested on the seventh day" clearly indicates that God finished working before Shabbat began. (There are some wonderful traditions in *Pirkei Avot* 5:8 about the things God created in the very moment before the first Shabbat began, such as manna and the tablets of the law.)

4. **Genesis 5:2 reads,** "Male and female He created them." When read in Hebrew, this verse could mean that Adam and Eve were separated at the very first moment of their creation, rather than Eve being formed from Adam's side, as is reported in Genesis 2:21–23. Steinsaltz suggests that the change in this verse was made to reconcile any confusion between the two versions of the creation story. That is, it clarifies that Adam alone was created first as a hermaphrodite, with both male and female characteristics. In one version it says *they* were created (plural) (here and Genesis 1:27), and in another (Genesis 1:27), *he* (Adam) was created (singular). The Jerusalem Talmud cites

a different change in this verse: "A man and his internal organs, He created them" (a small change in the Hebrew from *nekeivah*, נקיבה, to *nekuvav*, נקוביו). Again, the goal is the same: to make the text consistent with the rabbis' belief that man was created before woman.

The fact that the Torah contains two separate and different stories regarding the world's creation does not pose a problem for the rabbis. In the first version (Genesis 1:1–2:3), creation is accomplished in six days, humanity being created on the last day. Genesis 2:4–3:24 tells the story of creation in a quite different way. This version contains the tale of the serpent, the Tree of Life, and the curse upon Adam and Eve that they live by the sweat of the brow and bear their children with travail.

The rabbis theorized that God made and destroyed many worlds before God finally formed the world as we know it. According to the rabbis, instead of describing every attempt God made at creating the world, the first few chapters of Genesis simply provide us with descriptions of the last of these attempts.

5. **In the story of the Tower of Babel,** God says (Genesis 11:7), "Come, let *Us* go down and there confound their speech." This might lead one to believe that there is more than one Divine power, and so the sentence is changed from the plural to the singular form: "Come let *Me* descend and confound their tongues."

6. **When Sarah learns** that, at a very advanced age, she will bear a child, Genesis 18:12 reports, "And Sarah laughed within herself (*bekirbah*, בקרבה)." Changing this sentence from "within herself" to "among her relatives" is only a matter of adding a *vav* and a *yud* (*bikrovahah*, בקרוביה). This change answers the question, "If both Abraham and Sarah laughed when they heard that they would become parents at their advanced age (see Genesis 17:17 and Genesis 18:10–19), why is God angry only with Sarah and not with Abraham?" If Abraham only laughed inwardly at God's promise, but Sarah ridiculed it in public, this would explain the difference.

7. **In Jacob's final blessing to his sons,** he says of Shimon and Levi, "Let my soul not come into their council; to their

assembly let my honor not be united: for in their anger they slew a *man,* and in their willfulness they *lamed an ox*" (Genesis 49:6). The Septuagint changes this verse to, "For in their anger they slew an *ox* and in their wrath they *dug up a stall."* The changes made in this verse protect the honor of Jacob's sons so that they would not be called murderers. (Some commentators believe that Genesis 49:6 refers to Shimon's and Levi's murder of the people of Shechem's town after he raped their sister Dinah, and that the ox in this verse refers to the animals they took in their attack on that town. See Genesis 34:18–31.)

8. **When Moses returns to Egypt** to lead the children of Israel to freedom, the text states, "And Moses took his wife and his sons and set them upon an ass, and he returned to the land of Egypt" (Exodus 4:20). It seems that an ass was a lowly animal, and that it were better for such a great man to return to Egypt on a camel, which is how Rashi understands the phrase "carrier of men." This change may also reflect a change in the role of the camel in desert travel over time. The camel was not domesticated until approximately 1200 B.C.E. It is quite possible that everyone in Moses' day rode asses for desert travel, and thus the biblical text accurately reflects the history of Moses' day. However, when the rabbis wrote these translations, the camel may have become the animal of choice for desert travel, and they are simply making a change that reflects their own situation and what they assumed the situation was in more ancient times, as well.

9. **Exodus 12:40 states,** "Now the sojourning of the children of Israel who dwelt in Egypt was four hundred and thirty years." The translation states, "Now the time that the children of Israel dwelt in Egypt *and in other lands* was four hundred years." This change solves the following problem: if one counts the generations of the children of Israel in Egypt, one finds that they spent only 210 years there. However, they did spend 400 years in "lands not their own" (not just Egypt), which is what God foretold to Abraham during the covenant of the pieces (Genesis 15:7–20). God told Abraham (Genesis 15:13), "Know well that your offspring shall be strangers in a land not theirs,

and they shall be enslaved and oppressed four hundred years." This verse creates one additional problem. If one counts all the generations from this moment until the Exodus from Egypt, they come to 400 years, not 430. The rabbis resolve this problem by pointing out that God says to Abraham, "your offspring will spend 400 years in a land not their own," not "you (Abraham) will spend 400 years in a land not your own," and that it was thirty years from this moment to Isaac's birth. Therefore the prediction of four hundred years in exile was fulfilled.

10. **Exodus 24:5 reads,** "And he [Moses] sent the young men of the children of Israel and they offered burnt offerings, and sacrificed peace offerings of oxen to the Lord." This verse is set in the context of the revelation at Mount Sinai, when Moses sets up twelve pillars representing the twelve tribes of Israel and holds a solemn sacrificial ceremony during which the people of Israel agree to be bound by the Torah. One might wonder why young men would be sent to offer these sacrifices rather than more established leaders of the community. (In an analogous situation today, we might wonder if we attended a synagogue where only young people were given *aliyot* and honors during the service. Generally, we expect that leaders of the congregation, who are usually older, will be given these honors.) Therefore this verse is changed in order that more appropriate persons represent the people of Israel at this important moment.

However, it might be noted that if one wants to make a covenant, one's children are the best guarantors. *Song of Songs Rabbah* (chapter 1, section 4:1) relates the following dialogue between God and the children of Israel at Mount Sinai that dovetails nicely with the text as we have it in the Torah.

> When the people of Israel stood at Mount Sinai ready to receive the Torah, God said to them, "Bring Me good securities to guarantee that you will keep it, and then I will give the Torah to you."
> They said, "Our ancestors will be our securities."
> Said God to them, "I have faults to find with your ancestors . . . But bring Me good securities and I will give it to you."

They said, "King of the Universe, our prophets will be our securities."

He replied, "I have faults to find with your prophets. . . .
Still, bring Me good securities and I will give the Torah to you."

They said to Him, "Our children will be our securities."

And God replied, "Indeed these are good securities. For their sake I will give you the Torah."

11. **The verse Exodus 24:11,** "And upon the *nobles* [or leaders] of the children of Israel he laid not his hand," occurs in a passage that immediately follows the covenant ceremony described above. After the children of Israel bind themselves to the covenant with God, Moses, Aaron, Aaron's sons Nadav and Avihu, and seventy elders see God and eat and drink in God's presence. This is noteworthy, since directly seeing God was believed to cause death, and therefore God's presence is usually reported to be hidden in cloud and smoke. Here, however, seeing God does not harm these "nobles." Again, the idea of "elect ones" or "chosen persons" seems to better describe the rabbis' concept of the persons who participated in this feast than the category "nobles." Therefore, they change the word from "nobles" to "chosen ones." In addition, this change makes this verse consistent with their Greek version of Exodus 24:5, thus making the vocabulary of the story as a whole more uniform.

12. **In Numbers 16:15,** Moses speaks to God about his relationship with the rebels led by Korach. "I have not taken one ass from them," Moses asserts. The Septuagint changes the word *chamor* (*chet-mem-vav-reish,* חמור) to *chemed* (precious thing: *chet-mem-dalet,* חמד), a very small change in the Hebrew, which makes the sentence more inclusive and Moses' actions more honorable.

13. **Warning the children of Israel against idolatry,** Moses says, "And lest you lift up your eyes to heaven, and when you see the sun, and the moon, and the stars, all the host of heaven, you should be misled to worship them, and serve them, which the Lord Your God has allotted to all the nations under the whole heaven" (Deuteronomy 4:19). It is possible to

interpret this verse to mean that God gave the sun, moon, and stars to the nations *in order* that they should practice idolatry and worship them. The Septuagint adds "to give light," to make it clear that *this* was the reason God gave them, and for no other.

14. **God speaks in Deuteronomy 17:3,** saying, "And he went and served other gods and bowed to them, to the sun or to the moon or to any of the hosts of heaven, which I had not commanded." The problem solved by the Septuagint version of this verse is similar to that in number 13. It is possible to think that when God says, "which I had not commanded," it means God did not specifically create the moon or stars but that they created themselves (were gods unto themselves). To avoid this conclusion, the translation adds "which I commanded . . . should not be served."

All of these changes have to do with the core theme of this tractate: showing proper honor to God, Torah, and the people of Israel. Particularly striking is the defense of God's oneness, the core of Judaism. Of course, one might object that changing the Torah is no way to show it respect, and indeed none of the changes listed in this *sugyah* actually appear in the Septuagint we now have in our hands. That doesn't mean they didn't exist; it just means they are not in the manuscripts we have now. Regardless, we can see in these changes how the rabbis wished to guard against misunderstandings that could lead people to mistakenly give God less honor than God was due.

We now move into a very long section in which the rabbis demonstrate for us how to interpret the text on the level of *Drash*, expositions of the biblical text. They use the Book of Esther to demonstrate this technique and begin with fanciful introductions designed to pique our interest.

GEMARA (10b): Rabbi Joshua ben Levi introduced his discourse on this section with the following text: "And it shall come to pass that as the Lord rejoiced over you to do you good, so the Lord will rejoice over you to cause you to perish" (Deuteronomy 28:63). Now does the Holy One, blessed be He, rejoice in the downfall of the wicked? Is it not written, "As they went out before the army, and say, Give thanks unto the Lord, for His

mercy endures forever" (2 Chronicles 20:21) and Rabbi Johanan
said, "Why are the words 'for He is good' omitted from this
thanksgiving? Because the Holy One, blessed be He, does not
rejoice in the downfall of the wicked."

And Rabbi Johanan further said, What is the meaning of the
verse, "And one came not near the other all night" (Exodus
14:20)? The ministering angels wanted to chant their hymns, but
the Holy One, blessed be He, said, "The work of my hands is
being drowned in the sea, and shall you chant hymns?"

Rabbi Eleazar said, "He [God] does not rejoice, but does
cause others to rejoice." And this is precisely what is written,
"so He will cause to rejoice," not "and He will rejoice."

Today we expect a good speaker to begin his or her talk
with a joke or story and only slowly to embark on his or her
true topic. This is not a new technique. The rabbis who
composed the *midrashim* used this technique to begin their
sermons. However, instead of telling a joke or story, they
would amuse and inspire their congregations by posing a sort
of riddle or mystery. They would begin their sermon by
exploring a text that (apparently) has nothing to do with the
text at hand (in this case, the Book of Esther). Then, through a
series of intellectual and homiletical maneuvers, they would
end up connecting this first text with the second text. This
whole exercise is called a *petichah* (an opening or proem).

The *petichah* of Rabbi Joshua ben Levi immediately touches
on the theme of this whole tractate: the honor due individuals,
even evil ones. The text from Deuteronomy 28 actually seems
to imply that God rejoices when people perish. Is this an image
of God the rabbis are willing to accept? Yes and no. There are
some cases where they are willing to say that God avenges
wickedness. For example, the prayer the rabbis formulated for
the end of the *Megillah* reading praises God for the vengeance
meted out to the wicked (see Chapter 3 for more on this
subject). On the other hand, there is a strong tradition that saw
God as merciful and quite unwilling to rejoice when anyone,
no matter how evil, was destroyed.

This is the interpretation given to 2 Chronicles 20:21 (see 2
Chronicles 20:1–30). This section of Chronicles retells the
miraculous victory God gave Yehoshafat's army over the

armies of Moab and Ammon. Yehoshafat orders a chorus to sing the following song of praise to God as his army goes to battle: *Hodu l'Adonai, ki l'olam chasdo* ("Praise to God, for His steadfast love endures forever"). This song is missing the phrase *Hodu l'Adonai* ki tov, *ki l'olam chasdo* ("Praise to God, *for God is good,* for His steadfast love endures forever"), which appears in Psalms 107:1, 118:1, 29, 136:1, and 1 Chronicles 16:34. Therefore, it strikes the rabbis as odd that this verse in 2 Chronicles 20:21 should omit these two key words, *ki tov,* and they search for the meaning behind this omission. They believe this omission proves that we do not say that God is doing something good after the defeat of the enemy has already taken place and they lie dead before us. However, if we read the text in 2 Chronicles carefully, we find that this song and God's vanquishing of the enemy seem to happen simultaneously. Therefore the rabbis bring a stronger, more well-known *drash* to support their point.

This next *drash* refers to Exodus 14:20, a verse that describes the night before the Israelites flee from the Egyptians through the Red Sea where the Egyptians will drown (see Exodus 14:15–31). As part of the plan to deliver the Israelites, God sets a pillar of cloud between the Egyptian and Israelite camps, "so that *one did not come near the other* all night long." The simple meaning of the text seems to mean that the Egyptian and the Israelite camps were separated the whole night long.

The rabbis understand this phrase in a different light. They see the phrase *zeh el zeh* ("one to the other"), and it reminds them of the way the angels are described singing to one another in Isaiah 6:3. There it states, "And one cried to another *(v'kara zeh el zeh)* and said, 'Holy, holy, holy is the Lord of hosts: the whole earth is full of his glory'." Reading the phrase *zeh el zeh* ("one to another"), in both Isaiah and Exodus, the rabbis assumed that this phrase refers to angels in both texts. Therefore they assume that the phrase *zeh el zeh* in Exodus means that the *angels* did not draw near all the night before the parting of the Red Sea.

This raises the next question: Why wouldn't the angels come near one another on that night? Because they knew they should not rejoice when the Egyptians would soon be drowned. Of course, when we simply read the text of Exodus, we see no reference to angels, and the drowning of the Egyptians has yet to occur. These are not problematic issues for the rabbis. First, they felt that much of what happens in this world is paralleled in the heavenly spheres. For example, when we say "Holy, holy, holy" during our prayers, they believe the angels are saying it with us. Second, the rabbis felt that events in the Torah did not follow a strict chronology; they all occur simultaneously in a timeless realm. This principle *ein mukdam v'ein m'uchar baTorah*, literally, "there is no early or late in the Torah," is a central part of the way they regard the text.

So how do the rabbis solve the contradiction? In one text, Deuteronomy 28:63, God appears to rejoice in the downfall of the wicked. In the other two texts, 2 Chronicles 20:21 and Exodus 14:20, God does *not* rejoice at their downfall. Since we are to imitate God, should we or should we not rejoice when our enemies are defeated? And if we are not to rejoice at the downfall of our enemies, what would become of Purim, not to mention human nature? Rabbi Eleazar solves the problem elegantly by playing on the forms of the Hebrew verb "rejoice" here. *God* does not rejoice. However, God may *cause us* to rejoice in the downfall of our foes. This gets us away from the troublesome image of a vengeful, partisan God while still allowing us to feel happy when a foe has been defeated, as we do on Purim.

Having made their opening remarks, the rabbis now proceed to make *midrashim* directly on the text of Esther.

> **GEMARA (16a):** "And do even so to Mordecai the Jew, who sits at the king's gate, let nothing fail of all you have spoken" (Esther 6:10).
> He [Haman] said to him [Ahashueros], "Who is Mordecai?"
> He said to him, "The Jew."
> He said, "There are many Mordecais among the Jews."
> He said, "The one who sits in the king's gate."
> Said [Haman] to him, "For him [the tribute] of one village or one river is sufficient!"
> Said he [Ahasueros] to him [Haman], "Give him that too. 'Let nothing fail of all you have spoken.' "

This is one of the most common midrashic forms: the running *midrash* that explains apparently superfluous words. As we have noted before, the text of the *Tanach* is usually quite terse. When it is not, as here, the rabbis often supply dialogue to explain the seemingly extra words. This sentence (Esther 6:10) is spoken by Ahashueros immediately after Haman has described to him what should be done for the "man the king wishes to honor." Ahashueros could have simply said, "Do so for Mordecai." The continuation of the sentence, "the Jew, who sits at the king's gate, let nothing fail of all you have spoken," is, strictly speaking, unnecessary. Therefore the rabbis explain these phrases by supplying a dialogue that brought them about. This dialogue also shows how the rabbis viewed Haman as a selfish, greedy man who resisted honoring Mordecai.

A similar fill-in-the-blanks *midrash*, a much more famous one, is found in *Sanhedrin* 89b on Genesis 22:2, in which God uses a seemingly roundabout way of telling Abraham to sacrifice his son Isaac. Instead of simply saying, "Take Isaac," God says:

> "And God tested Abraham . . . and God said, 'Take, I pray you, your son, your only one, whom you love, Isaac' " (Genesis 22:1–2).
> "Your son"
> "[But] I have two sons!" [Abraham replied]
> "Your only one"
> "Each is the only one of his mother!"
> "Whom you love"
> "I love them both!"
> "Isaac."
> And why all this? [Why didn't God just say, "Take Isaac"?] So that his [Abraham's] mind would not reel [from the shock of hearing this command directly].

Another beautiful example of this method is a comment in *Yebamot* 47b on the famous declaration of loyalty Ruth makes to her mother-in-law, Naomi.

> He [a prospective convert] is not, however, to be persuaded or dissuaded too much [from choosing to become Jewish]. R.

Eleazar said: What is the scriptural proof? It is written, "And when she [Naomi] saw that she [Ruth] was steadfastly minded to go with her she left off speaking to her" (Ruth 1:18).

"We are forbidden," she [Naomi] said to her [Ruth], "[to move on the Sabbath beyond the] Sabbath boundaries!"

"Whither you go I will go" [Ruth replied](Ruth 1:16).

"We are forbidden private meeting between man and woman!"

"Where you lodge, I will lodge" (Ruth 1:16).

"We have been commanded six hundred and thirteen commandments!"

"Your people shall be my people" (Ruth 1:16).

"We are forbidden idolatry!"

"And your God, my God" (Ruth 1:16).

"Four modes of death were entrusted to the *Beit Din!*"

"Where you die, will I die" (Ruth 1:17).

"Two graveyards were placed at the disposal of the *Beit Din!*"

"And there will I be buried" (Ruth 1:17).

Presently "she saw that she was steadfastly minded to go with her, she left off speaking unto her" (Ruth 1:18).

As in the two other cases previously cited, this *midrash* explains what seem to be repetitions in Ruth's speech. Here, the dialogue reflects the rabbinic practice of teaching a prospective convert about Judaism. Note that Naomi, like the rabbis of the Talmud, points out the obligations that accrue to a Jew, so that Ruth will know what she faces. She will have to live with Sabbath restrictions, adopt a strict code of modesty, observe the commandments, forsake idolatry, and submit to the authority of the *Beit Din,* the Jewish court, which can sentence a person to death by any one of four methods (stoning, burning, slaying by the sword, and strangulation [see *Sanhedrin* 49b]), and command burial in two special cemeteries (one set aside for those whose death penalty was stoning or burning; the other for those executed by decapitation or strangulation). In this manner, the rabbis imbue Naomi with their own perspective and practice. This method of *midrash*-making is an easy one to start with when trying to interpret the *Tanach* midrashically.

The rabbis make a *drash* on a similar "superfluous" verse in the *Megillah*, Esther 8:16. (You might try this experiment:

Read Esther 8:15–17, then try it again, omitting verse 16, to see if the text flows without this verse.)

> **GEMARA (16b):** "The Jews had light and gladness and joy and honor" (Esther 8:16). Rav Judah said, "Light" means the Torah, and so it says, "For the commandment is a lamp and the Torah is light" (Proverbs 6:23).
>
> "Gladness" means a festival, and so it says, "And you shall be glad in your feast" (Deuteronomy 16:14).
>
> "Joy" means circumcision; and so it says, "I rejoice at your word" (Psalm 119:162).
>
> "Honor" means the phylacteries, and so it says, "And all the peoples of the earth shall see that the name of the Lord is called upon you, and they shall be afraid of you" (Deuteronomy 28:10).

First let us explain the simple meaning of each *drash*. The comparison of the Torah to light is clear, as is the association between gladness and festivals. The relationship of joy to circumcision is somewhat more complicated. First, the word "joy" (ששׂון) in the Esther verse is related to the word "rejoice" (שׂשׂ) in the Psalm verse. In addition, in Psalm 119:162, "word" (אמרתך) comes from the same root, *aleph-mem-reish* (אמר), as does the word "He (God) said" (ויאמר), which precedes the commandment to circumcise sons in Genesis 17:9. Therefore, the rabbis associate the "word" (אמרתך) in which we rejoice, which is mentioned in Psalm 119:162, with the "saying" (ויאמר) in Genesis 17:9.

When we look at Psalm 119:161, we get a clearer idea of why this verse might be interpreted as referring to circumcision. Psalm 119:161 says, "Princes have persecuted me without cause; but my heart stands in awe of Your word." Throughout the centuries, Jews have been persecuted for their observance of Jewish law. Circumcision has been prohibited, yet Jews have risked their lives to perform this *mitzvah*. By interpreting "joy" as "circumcision," the rabbis may be alluding to this persecution and devotion as a way of inspiring other generations to similar heights of piety.

Similarly, the phylacteries *(tefillin)* serve as a sign of the relationship between us and God, just as a wedding ring symbolizes the relationship between husband and wife. The link between the word "honor" (וִיקָר) and the verse from Deuteronomy is somewhat obscure. The rabbis may have associated the word "honor" (vikar, וִיקָר) with the word "called" (nikra, נִקְרָא) in Deuteronomy 28:10. They have two letters in common: kuph and reish (ק, ר). This may have been enough to draw the analogy between them. In addition, the tefillin that contain God's name, when worn, cause people to show honor to God by honoring the one who wears God's name upon his or her head. (Tefillin used to be worn all day long, and so served as a tangible association of God's name with a person.) This whole drash touches on the core issue of this chapter: the honor due those who observe the mitzvot and internalize Torah.

This whole drash is made possible because the verse Esther 8:16 is not strictly necessary for the story. Therefore, the rabbis feel it must be here to teach us something. They seem to attribute completely new meanings to the words in this verse, almost rewriting it to say, "The Jews had Torah and a festival, circumcision and tefillin."

Several commentators suggest that Haman may have decreed that the Jews were not allowed to study Torah, celebrate the holidays, perform circumcisions, or don tefillin. Indeed, any tyrant who has wanted to oppress the Jews has had to ban these forms of Jewish expression. These are some of the most basic mitzvot that unify the Jewish people and set us apart as a group. It may be no accident that this verse came to be used in the service of Havdalah, when we distinguish between all the dualities in our lives: the Shabbat and the rest of the week, light and darkness, and being Jewish in a non-Jewish world. Indeed, the meaning the rabbis give to the words in this verse are meanings that prevail against assimilation, that emphasize the uniqueness of the Jewish people.

The rabbis also show here their propensity for concretizing concepts. Light is not just any light, it is the light of Torah. Gladness is not just a happy feeling, but the joy of the festivals. This process of concretizing the abstract can be likened to two people relating to each other. One says, "I don't feel happy." Then the other attempts to find out what that means in concrete terms. "Does your stomach hurt? You don't want to go to the movies? You want to change jobs?" The former person is the Tanach text. The latter is the midrash.

The rabbis are able to make *midrashim* and see meaning even in the way the text is laid out in the scroll. At this point you may wish to look at a Torah scroll or *Megillah* for yourself. You can find the following distinctively written passages even in the tiny photocopied Torah scrolls given to children on Simchat Torah and in a *Tanach* written in Hebrew.

Try scrolling through the Torah, examining and identifying the passages that are laid out differently than the rest of the text. For example, look for the five-line spaces between the books of the Torah, the enlarged *bet* at the beginning of Genesis, the Song at the Sea (Exodus 15:1–19), the Ten Commandments (Exodus 20:1–14), the Priestly blessing (Numbers 6:24–26), the Ten Commandments (Deuteronomy 5:6–18), the *Shema* (Deuteronomy 6:4) (note the enlarged letters), the curses (Deuteronomy 27:15–26), and the poem *Ha'azinu* (Deuteronomy 32:1–43). You might also look in a Hebrew *Tanach* at these distinctively shaped portions: Joshua 12:9–24, Judges 5:1–31, 2 Samuel 22:1–51, and Ecclesiastes 3:1–8. The rabbis have their own explanations for these texts' forms.

> **GEMARA (16b):** All the songs [in Scripture] are written in the form of a half brick over a whole brick, and a whole brick over a half brick (e.g., Exodus 15:1–19) with the exception of this one (Esther 9:7–10) and the list of the kings of Canaan (Joshua 12:9–24), which are written in the form of a half brick over a half brick and a whole brick over a whole brick. What is the reason? So that they should never rise again from their downfall.

The rabbis interpret the format in which the names of Haman's sons are written in Esther 9:7–10 as significant. Instead of being laid out to look like a brick wall, as is the Song at the Sea (Exodus 15:1–19), the words of these verses form two straight columns. The rabbis interpret this formation to be an indication of Haman's sons' ultimate fate. Bricks laid directly atop one another are more likely to tumble than those laid out in the way one usually sees: half a brick over half a brick. Like the former brick wall, Haman and his sons are completely laid low, never to recover. Indeed, these sons of Haman were hanged together (and so their names are read in one breath during the *Megillah* reading). The list of the enemy kings of Canaan (Joshua 12:9–24) are written in a similar way, presumably for a similar reason. However, the poem *Ha'azinu* (Deuteronomy 32:1–43, which has 613 letters) is laid out in two parallel columns, as is Ecclesiastes 3:1–8, so the rabbis' reasoning here might not apply to every such biblical text, but only to lists of people.

As we come to the end of this first chapter, the rabbis emphatically restate the point they have been examining in it: Torah is the greatest source of honor.

> **GEMARA (16b):** Rav Joseph said: The study of the Torah is superior to the saving of lives . . .
>
> Rav—or some say, Rav Samuel bar Martta—said: The study of the Torah is superior to the building of the Temple . . .
>
> Rabbah said in the name of Rav Isaac bar Samuel bar Martta: The study of the Torah is superior to the honoring of father and mother.

This is a most surprising set of statements, indeed! Normally, *pikuach nefesh*, the saving of a life, takes precedence over all other *mitzvot* in Judaism. The rabbis may be saying that Torah—and here they may mean the intense spiritual transformation that takes place during Torah study—is the essence of living. Thus to study Torah is to save one's own life. To study Torah is equivalent to worshiping God in the Temple. To study Torah is the fulfillment of the heritage given to us by our parents, and thus studying it is the greatest way to show them love and honor.

In another passage from *Shabbat* 127a, familiar because it is contained in the preliminary morning worship service, the rabbis make this point in a less intense way:

> These are the things of which a person enjoys the fruits in this world, while the principal remains for him in the World to Come: honoring father and mother, practice of kindness, early attendance at the *Study House* morning and evening, hospitality to strangers, visiting the sick, dowering the bride, attending to the dead, devotion in prayer, and making peace between a person and his friend, and the study of Torah is worth all of them.

# 2

## The Text and the Soul

The categories we use to analyze a phenomenon can shape the way we experience it. For example, if we view a statue of a calf as a work of art, we will experience it one way. If we see it on the grounds of a milk farm, we may see it as an advertisement. If we see it in a pagan temple, we will experience it in a quite different way.

The rabbis now move from the direct encounter with the text, which they introduced us to in the first chapter, to viewing the text in a different context. In this chapter, they analyze our encounters with the text when we read it ritually. In tractate *Berachot*, they examined prayer by exploring how it was correctly accomplished, what could interfere with prayer, and so forth. They apply those same categories of correct recital and dealing with interferences here. But instead of applying these categories to prayers, they apply them to the experience of reciting the text in a ritual context.

The reading of the *Megillah* is likened to some of our most basic forms of worship: the recitation of the *Shema*, the *Hallel*, and the *Amidah* (*Megillah* 17a). The same issues that the rabbis address regarding the correct recital of those prayers are addressed in this chapter. For instance, note the similarities between the first *mishnah* in this chapter, which will be cited below, and the following one concerning the recitation of the *Shema* from tractate *Berachot* 15a.

If one recites the *Shema* without hearing what he says, he has
performed his obligation. Rabbi Jose says, he has not performed
his obligation.

If he recites it without pronouncing the letters correctly,
Rabbi Jose says that he has performed his obligation. Rabbi
Judah says that he has not performed his obligation.

If he recites it backward, he has not performed his obligation.

If he recites it and makes a mistake, he goes back to the place
where he made the mistake.

The following mishnah from *Berachot* 13a will also be echoed in
this chapter.

If one was reading in the Torah [the portion of the *Shema*]
when the time for its recital arrived, if he had the intention [to
fulfill that *mitzvah* in] his heart, he has performed his obligation.

The criteria used to judge an act of prayer valid are the same
criteria used to judge a ritual reading of a text: it must be
experienced with intensity, purpose, and with respect for the
text and the moment.

Having already taught us how to directly encounter the
text correctly in Chapter 1, the rabbis begin this chapter by
immediately dealing with factors that might interfere with that
encounter.

**MISHNAH (17a):** The one who reads the *Megillah* in the
wrong order has not performed his obligation. If he reads it by
heart, [or] if he read it in a translation in any language, he has
not performed his obligation. However, we read it to those who
do not understand Hebrew in a language other than Hebrew. If
one who does not understand Hebrew hears [it read] in Hebrew, he has performed his obligation. . . . If he was copying it,
correcting it or expounding it, then if he did it with the intention
[to fulfill his obligation to read the *Megillah*] then he has fulfilled
his obligation, but if not (if he did not read it with the intention
to fulfill his obligation) then he has not performed his obligation.

What is a correct recitation of the *Megillah*? The exact
words in the scroll should be read (not recited from memory) in

the exact way in which they were written, with the intention to fulfill the obligation of reading the *Megillah*. If you were sitting in synagogue on Purim and someone decided to read the *Megillah* starting with Chapter 10, then reading Chapter 9 and so forth, you wouldn't be able to follow the story. Likewise, if the reader recited the text from memory, even if you knew he or she had a great memory, you might wonder if they were saying it exactly right. In addition, you might be focusing more on the wonder of their memory rather than the wonder related in the story. Finally, if you had a scribe in your congregation and he was reading a *Megillah* scroll only in order to make sure there were no scribal errors in it, it would not have the same effect as one who read the *Megillah* for the purpose of celebrating the day and fulfilling the *mitzvah*.

The rabbis seem to be ambivalent on the issue of reading the *Megillah* in translation. It is interesting that while we tend to think of the problem of illiteracy in Hebrew as a modern problem, the rabbis of the *Mishnah* obviously had to deal with this issue. How did they solve it? In their characteristic, see-both-sides-of-an-issue way. It is preferable to read the *Megillah* in Hebrew. However, it is more important to have the listeners understand the story than to simply read it in Hebrew. So they compromise. If one hears the *Megillah* read in Hebrew, but does not understand it, one has still fulfilled one's duty to hear the *Megillah* read on Purim. However, it is better to understand what has been read.

Today texts and prayers are read in Hebrew to many congregations composed largely of persons who do not understand the language. Congregants may feel the same ambivalence the rabbis expressed: they like to hear the liturgy in Hebrew, but they also want to understand what is being said. Until universal Hebrew literacy has been achieved, we may be guided by the rabbis' decision: there is something uplifting in hearing the words in Hebrew, even when we do not understand them.

Can one truly stand in the chain of tradition if one does not know Hebrew? Of course, every person, as well as every community, must make this decision for themselves. There is no doubt that knowing Hebrew is like knowing a shortcut to

Jewish insights. It's similar to the difference between taking a highway to a destination as opposed to side streets. Using the highway gets you to your destination quickly and smoothly. Traveling the side streets takes more time, and you might get lost more easily. If you know Hebrew, coming to the core of Jewish knowledge will be a swifter and easier process than if you do not. However, you can still reach your destination, and it may even be by a more scenic route than you'd otherwise have traveled, if you do not know Hebrew. Yet just knowing Hebrew is not enough to bring one closer to tradition. There are many Israelis who speak Hebrew who will tell you that they are not particularly interested in the Jewish tradition. In other words, you still have to steer the car, even if you're on the freeway.

In the next *sugyah,* the rabbis move on to directly relate text to prayer. This *sugyah* is long, and sometimes difficult. Therefore, it will be helpful for you to read the entire text of the *Amidah* from a traditional prayer book, and read Psalm 29, before you begin. In addition, you might want to count the number of times God's name is mentioned in this psalm. To understand this *sugyah,* we must be familiar with the structure of the *Amidah,* the prayer par excellence. On weekdays, it is made up of nineteen benedictions, recited in the order outlined below. At one time this prayer consisted of only eighteen benedictions, and it is called the *Shemoneh Esrei* (the Eighteen Benedictions) to this day, even though it generally contains nineteen benedictions.

*First Three Blessings*
1. *Avot* ("Fathers," אבות)
2. *Gevurot* ("God's Might," גבורות)
3. *Kedushat HaShem* ("The Holiness of God's name," קדושת השם) (contains the *Kedushah* in the morning and afternoon services).

*Weekday Petitions*
Individual Petitions
4. *Da'at* ("Knowledge," דעת) *(Havdalah)*
5. *Teshuvah* ("Repentance," תשובה)
6. *Selichah* (Forgiveness, סליחה)

7. *Geulah* ("Redemption," נאולה) (Prayer for Fast Days)
8. *Refuah* ("Healing," רפואה)
9. *Birkat HaShanim* ("The Blessing of the Year" [for food], ברכת השנים)

Communal Petitions

10. *Kibbuts Galuyot* ("Ingathering of the Exiles," קבוץ גלויות)
11. *Hashavat HaMishpat* ("The Return of Justice," השבת המשפט)
12. *Birkat HaMinim* ("The Blessing of the Heretics," ברכת המנים)
13. *Al HaTsadikim* ("[Blessing for] the Righteous Ones," על הצדיקים)
14. *Binyan Yerushalayim* ("The Building of Jerusalem," בנין ירושלים)
15. *Mashiach ben David* ("Messiah son of David," משיח בן דוד)
16. *Shomeia Tefillah* ("[God who] Hearkens to Prayer," שומע תפלה)

**OR**
*Prayers for Shabbat and Holidays*

*Final Three Blessings*

17. *Avodah* ("[Prayer for acceptance of prayer and] Sacrifice," עבודה) (Intermediate days of a festival)
18. *Hoda'ah* ("Thanks," הודאה) (Hanukkah) (Purim)
19. *Birkat Shalom* ("The Blessing of Peace," ברכת שלום)
    *Shalom Rav* (evening and afternoon)
    *Sim Shalom* (morning)
    The Priestly Benediction may be included here

Just as the *mishnah* above tells us that the *Megillah* must be recited in the correct order, so must the *Hallel, Shema,* and *Amidah* be said in their set order in order to be correctly recited. The order for the blessings in the *Amidah* is logical and meaningful. We make our connection with God in the first three prayers. First we remind God that we are descendants of the Patriarchs, with whom God had an especially close relationship *(Avot).* Then we praise God's might *(Gevurot).* We then affirm that we are in a special, holy, and mutually binding relationship, similar to a marriage, with God *(Kedushat HaShem)*. After we have made this connection with God, we can then petition God for our needs. These weekday petitions fall in a logical order. First we pray for understanding *(Da'at*, also called *Binah)*, for we must have the understanding to know how to pray. Our understanding brings us to the knowledge that we may have sinned and need to repent before we can make petitions *(Teshuvah)*. When we repent, we can be satisfied that God forgives *(Selichah)*. Having repented and been forgiven, we can ask for redemption *(Geulah)*, healing *(Refuah)*, and rain (i.e., food in abundance) *(Birkat HaShanim)*. Once we have asked for our individual needs, our thoughts turn to the community, and we petition for national redemption *(Kibbuts Galuyot)* and the reestablishment of justice *(Hashavat HaMishpat)*, punishment for the wicked *(Birkat HaMinim)*, rewards for the righteous *(Al Ha-Tsadikim)*, the rebuilding of Jerusalem *(Binyan Yerushalayim)*, and the return of the rule of King David's house there *(Mashiach ben David)*. Finally, we praise God for listening to our prayers *(Shomeia Tefillah)*. Then, in the last three benedictions, we ask God to accept our prayer and for the return of the sacrifices to the Temple *(Avodah)*, we say thank You to God *(Hoda'ah)*, and having done so, we feel at peace *(Birkat Shalom)*.

This order is so logical that there would seem little need to justify it by relating it to texts from the Tanach and to the practice of Judaism. However, there are powerful reasons to relate the experiencing of text to the experience of prayer, which is what the rabbis accomplish in the following *sugyah*. First, let us go through the basic meaning of this *sugyah* before we examine its broader significance. Because the text of this *sugyah* is so lengthy, brief commentaries on each section are interspersed within the text itself. The Talmud text is indented.

GEMARA (17b): [The *Megillah* is likened to the] Tefillah (i.e., the *Amidah*). Whence is this derived? As it has been taught: Simeon the Pakulite formulated the eighteen blessings in the presence of Rabban Gamaliel in the proper order in Yavneh. Rabbi Johanan said (others report, it was stated in a *Baraita*): A hundred and twenty elders, among whom were many prophets, drew up eighteen blessings in a fixed order.

> Our rabbis taught: Whence do we derive that the blessing of
> the Patriarchs should be said? Because it says, "Ascribe unto the
> Lord, O you sons of might" (Psalm 29:1).

Let us examine this first paragraph sentence by sentence.
First, the *Megillah* is likened to the *Tefillah* in that both must be
said in their proper order. This leads the rabbis to the topic of
the proper order of the blessings in the *Tefillah* and how they
were determined. There seems to be some confusion on this
point. One tradition holds that Simeon the Pakulite formulated
the blessings in their correct order in Yavneh, a town in Judea
where the sages met between approximately 70–135 C.E. to
formulate a uniform Jewish practice that could survive the
Temple's destruction. However, another tradition maintains
that the *Tefillah* was established by the Men of the Great
Assembly. The prophets referred to may be the last prophets
Haggai, Zecharia, and Malachi. In other words, one theory
suggests the order of the prayers in the *Amidah* was developed
at a rather late date; the other at a rather early one. These
different theories will be reconciled at the end of the *sugyah*.
However, the Gemara now embarks on a very lengthy discussion of each of the prayers in the *Amidah*, linking them to texts
from *Tanach* and/or Jewish practices.
    The prayer *Avot* ("The Patriarchs") is linked to Psalm 29:1,
"Ascribe to the Lord, O you mighty (literally, 'sons of might')."
The rabbis equate "sons of might" with the Patriarchs Abraham, Isaac, and Jacob mentioned in the *Avot*.

> And whence that we say the blessing of mighty deeds?
> Because it says, "Ascribe unto the Lord glory and *strength*" (Psalm
> 29:1).

The second blessing, *Gevurot*, which praises God's might, is
also related to Psalm 29:1. Strength in the psalm verse is related
to God's might, which is recounted in the *Tefillah*'s second
blessing.

> And whence that we say the sanctifications? Because it says,
> "Ascribe unto the Lord the glory due His name, worship the
> Lord in the beauty of *holiness (kodesh)*" (Psalm 29:2).

The third blessing, the *Kedushah* (קדושה), in which we proclaim God's holiness, is linked to the next verse in Psalm 29 through the related words *kodesh* (קודש, "holiness" in Psalm 29:2), and *Kedushah* ("Sanctification") the name of this prayer. For the rabbis, the important thing for "drashing," or relating two texts, is that each text has a word derived from the same root letters. The actual word need not be the same in each verse, if they share a common root. It would be much the same if you wanted to compare forms of the verb "to go" in different sentences in English. One sentence might have the word "going" in it, while another might have "went," and yet another could contain the word "gone." However, you would still be able to compare the sentences, since they all contained forms of the same verb. Here, since both the third blessing of the *Tefillah* and this third phrase in Psalm 29 both have words derived from the root *kuph-dalet-shin* (קדש), the rabbis are able to relate them to each other.

> What reason had they for mentioning understanding after holiness? Because it says, "They shall sanctify (*hikdishu*, הקדישו) the Holy One of Jacob and shall stand in awe of the God of Israel (Isaiah 29:23ff)." And next to this, "And they that err in spirit shall come to understanding (*binah*, בינה)."

In the forth blessing, we ask for *binah* (בינה, "understanding"). Here, the rabbis explain that this blessing is placed after the Sanctification because in Isaiah 29:23–24 the sanctification of God's name is followed by the acquiring of understanding.

The rabbis will now search for an appropriate proof text to explain the order of the next four blessings: Repentance (*Teshuvah*), Forgiveness (*Selichah*), Redemption (*Geulah*), and Healing (*Refuah*).

> What reason had they for mentioning repentance after understanding? Because it is written, "Lest they, understanding (*yavin*, יבין) with their heart, return (*vashav*, ושב) and be healed (*v'rafa*, ורפא)" (Isaiah 6:10). If that is the reason, healing should be mentioned after repentance? Do not imagine such a thing, since it is written, "And let him return (*v'yashav*, וישב) unto the Lord

and he will have compassion upon him, and to our God, for he will abundantly pardon (*lisloach,* לסלוח)" (Isaiah 55:7). But why should you rely on this verse? Rely rather on the other! There is written another verse, "Who forgives (*hasoleiach,* הסלח) all your iniquity, who heals (*harofei,* הרפא) all your diseases, who redeems (*hago-eil,* הגואל) your life from the pit" (Psalm 103:3ff), which implies that redemption and healing come after forgiveness. But it is written, "Lest they return and be healed (Isaiah 6:10)"? That refers not to the healing of sickness but to the healing [power] of forgiveness.

What was their reason for mentioning redemption in the seventh blessing? Rava said: Because they [Israel] are destined to be redeemed in the seventh year [of the coming of the Messiah], therefore the mention of redemption was placed in the seventh blessing. But a Master has said, "In the sixth year will be thunderings, in the seventh wars, at the end of the seventh the son of David will come." War is also the beginning of redemption.

What was their reason for mentioning healing in the eighth blessing? Rabbi Aha said: Because circumcision which requires healing is appointed for the eighth day, therefore it was placed in the eighth blessing.

The rabbis seem to be searching for just the right proof text to explain the order of the next blessings. They would like to use the Isaiah 6:10 verse, in which the root *bet-yud-nun,* from which the word "understanding" is formed, is followed by the root *shin-vav-bet,* from which the word "repentance" comes, thereby corresponding to the order of the blessings. This text is problematic, however, because it ends with a word whose root is *reish-pey-aleph* (כ-פ-א, "healing"), and the prayer for healing does not follow the prayer for repentance in the *Tefillah.* Therefore, they cite another text, Isaiah 55:7, in which a word with the root *shin-vav-bet* (ש-ו-ב) is followed by a word with the root *samech-lamed-chet* (ס-ל-ח), with the root meaning of "forgiveness." This text from Isaiah 55:7 apparently provides a satisfactory explanation of the order of the prayers for Repentance and Forgiveness. However, the rabbis have still not settled on a text that explains the order of the blessing of Forgiveness and Healing. So yet another text, Psalm 103:3ff., is suggested, which supplies a word with the root *samech-lamed-chet* (ס-ל-ח,

forgiveness), followed by a word with the root *reish-peh-aleph* (ר-פ-א, healing) and then a word regarding redemption (*hago'eil*, הגואל, corresponding to the blessing for Redemption, גאולה.) The rabbis may have had a problem with this verse, though, because it mentions (1) forgiveness, (2) healing, and (3) redemption, rather than giving them in the order in which they are found in the *Tefillah*: (1) forgiveness, (2) redemption, and (3) healing. Therefore, this proof text is not appropriate for use as an explanation of the order of the blessings in the *Tefillah*. So the rabbis return to the verse from Isaiah 6:10, in which *teshuvah* was followed directly by healing. The rabbis reconcile this verse with the order of blessings in the *Tefillah* by stating that the healing Isaiah refers to is a healing of the spirit, not the body, and is thus equivalent to forgiveness. This interpretation of Isaiah 6:10 provides a text that explains the order of the blessings in which the blessing for Repentance precedes the blessing for Forgiveness.

Why does the blessing for redemption follow the blessing for forgiveness, rather than the blessing for healing, especially since Psalm 103:3ff. "Who forgives all your iniquity, who *heals* all your diseases, who *redeems* your life from the pit" seems to imply that that would be the correct order? Because tradition teaches that the ultimate redemption of the Jewish people will come in the sabbatical year for the land, the seventh year of the agricultural cycle outlined in Leviticus. An objection is raised that the wars preceding the Messiah's arrival will occur in the seventh year, and only at the end of that year will the Messiah arrive. However, the rabbis assert that these wars are the beginning of the redemption, and so the explanation holds good. Interestingly, here the rabbis shift from relating each blessing to a text, to relating blessings to either a text *or* a Jewish practice or belief. Either the rabbis could not find a suitable text linking the number seven to redemption, or the concept mentioned above was foremost in their minds.

Healing is mentioned as the eighth blessing because circumcision, which requires healing, occurs on the eighth day of life. Also, just as healing is the combined art of God's and humans' efforts to control nature, so circumcision is the combined efforts of humanity and God to make from what occurs naturally (birth with a foreskin) a holy covenant (circumcision).

> What was their reason for placing the [prayer for the] blessing of the years ninth? Rabbi Alexandri said: This was directed against those who raise the market price [of foodstuffs], as it is written, "Break you the arm of the wicked" (Psalm 10:15), and when David said this, he said it in the ninth Psalm.

The rabbis suggest that the blessing for the years, in which we request rain so that there should be no famine, was placed ninth in the *Amidah* as a rebuke to those who extorted money for grain in years when rain was not plentiful. They relate this placement of the blessing to the placement of the verse from Psalms in Psalm 9. However, today we find this verse in Psalm 10, not Psalm 9. Verses 8–9 of Psalm 10 vividly describe the wicked person who takes advantage of the poor in a year of famine: "He sits in the lurking places of the villages, in the secret places he murders the innocent. His eyes stealthily watch for the helpless. He lies in wait secretly like a lion in his den. He lies in wait to catch the poor. He catches the poor, when he draws him into his net." This connection between those who sell the harvest for inflated prices and the ninth blessing might be difficult to understand, were it not that it hints at another similar *midrash* on the order of the *Tefillah's* benedictions. That midrash on Psalm 29 makes each mention of God's name in the psalm correspond to a blessing of the *Tefillah*. Halivni (1974) shows how this explanation of the ninth blessing's position in the *Tefillah* was transferred from one place in the tradition to another. This process of ferreting out how different traditions were incorporated into the *Gemara* text as we have it now is an important part of scholarly investigations into how the Talmud was composed. Psalm 29:5 contains the ninth mention of God's name in the psalm and reads: "The voice of the Lord breaks cedars." The *Midrash on Psalms* comments:

> Next, "The voice of the Lord breaks cedars" calls for the benediction, "Blessed are You . . . who blesses the years." The

men who raise prices and give small measure, and the rich men
who live in plenty and appear strong as cedars—such men the
Lord breaks to bits when He blesses His world by bringing low
prices to it, thereby breaking the staff of wickedness. Hence, the
verse calls for the benediction, "Blessed are You . . . who blesses
the years."

This seems to make a more natural connection between the
punishment of unethical businessmen and the ninth blessing.
(See the end of this chapter for the entire *midrash* on Psalm 29.)
This *drash* on the ninth blessing of the *Amidah* also tells us
about the economic life of the people who originally made this
*midrash:* those who charged exorbitant prices for food were
looked on with wrath, yet the people were apparently power-
less against them. They had to rely on God to drive down the
price of food by providing rain, thus ruining these immoral
traders.

What was their reason for mentioning the gathering of the
exiles after the blessing of the years? Because it is written, "But
you, O mountains of Israel, you shall shoot forth your branches
and yield your fruit to My people Israel, for they are at hand to
come" (Ezekiel 36:8).

This *drash* seems to imply that once the year has been blessed
and an abundant harvest is at hand and the land will be filled
with abundant food ("yield fruit to My people Israel"), then the
people of Israel will come near, that is, be gathered in. With
this blessing, we start a section of the *Amidah* (blessings ten
through sixteen) that could also be interpreted as a step-by-step
description of the manner in which the rabbis believed the
Messiah will come. First the exiles will be gathered to the Land
of Israel. Then courts of justice will be reestablished that will
punish the wicked and reward the righteous. Jerusalem will be
rebuilt and the Messiah, descended from David, will preside
over the City of Peace, and our prayers will be heard and
answered from that time forth.

And when the exiles are assembled, judgment will be visited
on the wicked as it says, "And I will turn my hand upon you and

purge away your dross as with lye" (Isaiah 1:25), and it is written further, "And I will restore your judges as at the first" (Isaiah 1:26).

This is a straightforward *midrash* explaining why the blessing for the Return of Judgment follows the blessing for the Ingathering of the Exiles. The quote from Isaiah depicts God purging away the dross of the people, that is, executing justice on sinners. The Hebrew of this verse, in a slightly different grammatical form, is even the Hebrew phrasing used in this blessing, which begins, "Restore our judges as at first . . ."

> And when judgment is visited on the wicked, transgressors cease, and presumptuous sinners are included with them, as it is written, "But the destruction of the transgressors and of the sinners shall be together, and they that forsake the Lord shall be consumed" (Isaiah 1:28).

The judgment referred to here is not just of criminals and evildoers, as is the judgment mentioned in the immediately preceding blessing. This is a special judgment on "presumptuous sinners,"—apostates from Judaism. The Blessing of the Heretics requests that these apostates be totally destroyed.

> And when the transgressors have disappeared, the horn of the righteous is exalted, as it is written, "All the horns of the wicked also will I cut off, but the horns of the righteous shall be lifted up" (Psalm 75:11). And "proselytes (*gerei,* גרי) of righteousness" are included with the righteous, as it says, "You shall rise up before the hoary head and honor the face of the old man (Leviticus 19:32)" and next to it [it says], "And if a stranger (*ger,* גר) sojourn with you [in your land, you shall not do him wrong.]" (Leviticus 19:33).

This next blessing is the opposite of the two that preceded it. While those asked for judgment on the wicked and the annihilation of apostates from Judaism, this blessing asks for rewards for the righteous, especially mentioning righteous proselytes to Judaism. The annihilation of the transgressors allows the righteous, including righteous converts, to flourish. These two groups of righteous persons are linked together through the verses from Leviticus. There, honor is shown to an old man who, the rabbis presumed, had learned much Torah in his life and was thus righteous, and directly following this a *ger* (גר) is mentioned. In Hebrew the word *ger* (גר) can refer to either a convert or a stranger. In the simple meaning of the biblical text, the word probably means the latter. However, Leviticus 19:33–34 lends itself to both interpretations:

> And if a *ger* (stranger *or* righteous convert) sojourn with you in your land, you shall not wrong him. But the *ger* (stranger *or* righteous convert) that dwells with you shall be to you as one born among you, and you shall love him as yourself, for you were strangers in the Land of Egypt: I am the Lord your God.

The word *horn* in the context of this blessing is probably best understood as "future." So it is the future of the wicked that is to be cut off and the future of the righteous that shall be lifted up. Likewise, in the next blessing, the word *horn* again can be understood as "future."

> And where is the horn of the righteous exalted? In Jerusalem, as it says, "Pray for the peace of Jerusalem, may they prosper that love you" (Psalm 122:6).

The future of the righteous is in Jerusalem, and so the next blessing of the *Tefillah* asks for the rebuilding of that city. The rabbis apparently assume that all who love Jerusalem are righteous and should prosper and be exalted. To truly understand this proof text, we must look at Psalm 122 as a whole. It could easily be taken as a vision of the rebuilding of Jerusalem by the righteous in the messianic era.

> A Song of Ascents; of David. I rejoiced when they said unto me: "Let us go unto the house of the Lord [the Temple]." Our feet are standing within your gates, O Jerusalem. Jerusalem, that is built as a city that is compact together. Whither the tribes went up, even the tribes of the Lord, as a testimony to Israel, to give thanks unto the name of the Lord. For there were set thrones for judgment, the thrones of the house of David. Pray for the peace of Jerusalem; may they prosper that love you. Peace be within your walls, and prosperity within your palaces.

For my brethren and companions' sakes I will now say: "Peace be within you." For the sake of the house of the Lord our God I will seek your good.

The verse (122:6) from this psalm may also have been used as a proof text here because the reestablishment of justice is portrayed as taking place in Jerusalem, which also corresponds to the order of the blessings in the *Tefillah*. Once Jerusalem has been rebuilt—that is, once a proper throne has been prepared—David (that is, the Messiah, who will be a descendant of the Davidic line) will rule over the rebuilt city.

> And when Jerusalem is built, David will come, as it says (18a), "Afterwards shall the children of Israel return and seek the Lord their God, and David their king" (Hosea 3:5).

The return of the children of Israel refers to their return to Jerusalem. Once they have returned and reconstituted a system of justice that seeks to follow God's ways, then David, or a descendant of David, will arrive to rule over them.

> And when David comes, prayer will come, as it says, "I will bring them to my holy mountain, and make them joyful in my house of prayer (*tefillati*, תפלתי). (Isaiah 56:7)"

Once the Messiah arrives, the Jewish people will be united in prayer (*tefillah*, תפלה). Therefore, the blessing praising God for answering prayer is placed after the one regarding the Messiah in the *Amidah*. The proof text from Isaiah indicates that the righteous will be brought to the Temple Mount ("my holy mountain") and rejoice in the (rebuilt) house of prayer (the Temple).

> And when the prayer has come, the Temple service [i.e., the sacrifices] will come, as it says, "Their burnt offerings and their sacrifices shall be acceptable upon my altar" (Isaiah 56:7).

Once the Temple has been rebuilt, then the system of sacrifices will be reinstituted. The rabbis may assume that the first thing we would pray for after the Messiah comes, and therefore the first prayer granted, would be for the reestablishment of the Temple cult.

> And when the service [the sacrifices] comes, thanksgiving will come, as it says, "Whoso offers praise glorifies Me" (Psalm 50:23).

The verse from Psalms and the order of the blessings in the *Tefillah* imply that once sacrifices have been offered in the reestablished Temple, thanks will immediately be offered. Some commentators feel that the thanks are verbal, others that this verse from Psalms refers to an additional sacrifice of thanksgiving given after the other sacrifices. They translate this verse "Whoso offers *the sacrifice of thanksgiving* honors me." Both interpretations correspond to the order of the blessings in the *Tefillah:* sacrifices are followed by thanksgiving.

> What was their reason for inserting the priestly benediction after thanksgiving? Because it is written, "And Aaron lifted up his hands toward the people and he came down from offering the sin offering and the burnt offering and the peace offerings" (Leviticus 9:22). But cannot I say that he did this before the service? Do not imagine such a thing. For it is written, "and he came down *from* offering." Is it written "*to* offer"? It is written "*from* offering." Why not then say it [the priestly benediction] after the [blessing of] the Temple service? Do not imagine such a thing, since it is written, "whoso offers the sacrifice of thanksgiving" (Psalm 50:23). Why base yourself upon this verse? Why not upon the other? It is reasonable to regard service and thanksgiving as one.
> What was their reason for having "give peace" said after the priestly benediction? Because it is written, "So they [the priests] shall put my name upon the children of Israel, and [then] I shall bless them" (Numbers 6:27) and the blessing of the Holy One blessed be He, is peace, as it says, "The Lord shall bless His people with peace" (Psalm 29:11).

The Priestly Benediction (Numbers 6:24–26) may be said at this juncture in the *Tefillah* during a synagogue service. The rabbis base this practice on the verse from Leviticus 9, but this verse itself is subject to different interpretations. First it mentions Aaron raising his hands toward the people, and then it mentions the sacrifices. This raising of hands by the priests is assumed to be the performance of the Priestly Benediction. (This benediction is bestowed with hands held over the congregation to this day.) So did Aaron bless the people first and then perform the sacrifices, as it might appear from the order of this verse? Or did he perform the sacrifices and then bless the people? Since the verse mentions the blessing first, we might think it preceded the sacrifices. However, it is clear from the verse's context that Aaron offered the sacrifices first (see Leviticus 9:1–21) and then blessed the people.

The rabbis then seem to wonder why the Priestly Benediction is offered after the thanksgiving and not before it. They therefore hearken back to verse 23 from Psalm 50, which they already took as conclusive proof that the thanksgiving sacrifices were offered immediately after the other sacrifices were offered.

To determine why the blessing of peace comes last in the *Tefillah*, the rabbis referred to the description of the Priestly Benediction, Numbers 6:22–27:

> And the Lord spoke to Moses, saying, "Speak to Aaron and to his sons, saying, In this way you shall bless the children of Israel, saying to them, 'The Lord bless you and keep you. The Lord make His face to shine upon you and be gracious to you. The Lord lift up his countenance to you, and give you peace.' And they shall put My name upon the children of Israel and I will bless them."

The rabbis assumed that the order of events mentioned in the Torah would be the order in which the actual blessings were bestowed at all times. First the priests would recite the benediction over the people, *then* God would grant blessing upon them. God's greatest gift, and the last gift mentioned in the Priestly Benediction, is peace, and is therefore the last blessing of the *Tefillah*.

This placement of the blessing for peace may also relate to the last verse of Psalm 29, which ends with the word *peace:*

"The Lord gives strength to his people; the Lord blesses His people with peace." Our *sugyah* concludes with the following summation:

> Seeing now that a hundred and twenty elders, among whom were many prophets, drew up the prayers in the proper order, why did Simeon the Pakulite formulate them? They were forgotten, and he formulated them afresh.

Just as Jonathan ben Uzziel only wrote down in his translation what had been formulated centuries before by the prophets (page 3a), so here, Simeon the Pakulite is said to be merely reviving rituals of ancient origins. Of course, it could also be that he formulated this order himself and attributed it to an earlier generation, as was suggested at the beginning of our *sugyah*. There it was stated that Simeon the Pakulite formulated this order of the blessings at Yavneh. Both statements could be correct. The Men of the Great Assembly might well have formulated these blessings, but they could have fallen into disuse, remembered by only a few individuals. They might then have been reinstituted at Yavneh, when the Jewish people needed a uniform system of prayer.

We see examples of this sort of ebb and flow in Jewish life all the time. For example, at the beginning of the twentieth century, when Jews came to America, many of them threw off all visible signs of their Jewish identity. Their *kipot* (skullcaps) and *tsitsit* (ritual fringes) were abandoned. These Jews wanted to appear as purely American as possible. Only a relatively small number of American Jews continued to wear their *kipot* and *tsitsit*. Now many Jews are returning to tradition and are again wearing *kipot* and *tsitsit*. In the process, they may turn to those Jewish communities that never abandoned the customs for guidance on the adoption of these *mitzvot*. Such preservation of diverse practices within the Jewish community is one source of its flexibility and strength.

Now that we have grasped the straightforward meaning of this *sugyah*, we may ask, "Why is this *sugyah* here?" If we excise this long section linking the prayers of the *Tefillah* to different texts and Jewish practices, we see that the *sugyah* would have flowed quite nicely without it.

[The *Megillah* is likened to the] *Tefillah* (i.e., the *Amidah*). Whence is this derived? As it has been taught: Simeon the Pakulite formulated the eighteen blessings in the presence of Rabban Gamaliel in the proper order in Yavneh. Rabbi Johanan said (others report, it was stated in a *Baraita*): A hundred and twenty elders, among whom were many prophets, drew up eighteen blessings in a fixed order. . . .

Seeing now that a hundred and twenty elders, among whom were many prophets, drew up the prayers in the proper order, why did Simeon the Pakulite formulate them? They were forgotten, and he formulated them afresh.

Why is this long *sugyah* here, in Tractate *Megillah,* instead of in Tractate *Berachot,* which has two whole chapters devoted to the *Tefillah?* It could have been inserted into the following discussion of the *Tefillah* in tractate *Berachot* quite logically.

BERACHOT (28b): To what do these Eighteen Benedictions correspond? Rabbi Hillel the son of Rabbi Samuel bar Nahmani said, "To the eighteen times that David mentioned the Divine Name in the Psalm [which begins], 'Ascribe unto the Lord, O ye sons of might' " (Psalm 29). Rav Joseph said, "To the eighteen times the Divine Name is mentioned in the Recitation of the *Shema.*" Rabbi Tanhum said in the name of Rabbi Joshua ben Levi, "To the eighteen vertebrae in the spinal column." . . . (The *sugyah* could be inserted here.)

This long *sugyah* relating the *Tefillah* to texts and Jewish practices seems to have been placed here in this tractate, in this chapter, for a definite purpose. It may have been to underscore the theme of this chapter: the examination of encounters with the text that involve the feelings, thoughts, and the spirit of prayer. The rabbis could have included this *sugyah* in this chapter to show that the midrashic process, which they fully demonstrated in relation to the Book of Esther in Chapter 1, can be applied to other texts and to prayer, as well. In addition, they may be hinting that the process of making *midrashim* and deeply encountering the text shares many characteristics with prayer, such as deep intention, joy, and awe.

We must also ask ourselves why the rabbis offer the

midrash we read above rather than the running *midrash* on Psalm 29, of which they seem to have been aware. They may have had subtle, important reasons for their choice. The *midrash* on Psalm 29 is attributed to Moses, whereas the *sugyah* we have here is attributed to the rabbis in relation to 120 elders and/or Simeon the Pakulite. The rabbis may have wanted to demonstrate their idea that Judaism is a realm where everything, every text, is connected to every other text in a timeless way. Linking the *Tefillah* to just one psalm and just one authority (Moses) would not drive that point home as well as this *sugyah*, in which the *Tefillah* is linked to various texts, Jewish practices, things that are to happen in the future, and things that happened in the past.

This *sugyah* teaches us a very holistic way of looking at prayer, text, and life. They aren't airtight categories that can be neatly separated one from the other. Rather, they feed one another: the more text you know, the more Jewishly you live your life, the more sincere your prayer will be. The more Jewishly you live your life and the more sincere your prayer is, the more you will bring to your study of text. The more text you know and the more sincere your prayer, the more Jewishly you will end up living your life.

The rabbis continue their examination of the relationship between text and prayer, coming to a mystical, paradoxical, conclusion.

> **GEMARA (18a):** Beyond this [the benedictions in the *Tefillah* set by the 120 elders] it is forbidden to declare the praise of the Holy One, blessed be He. . . .
>
> Rabbi Judah a man of Kefar Gibboraya, or as some say, of Kefar Gibbor Hayil, expounded: What is meant by the verse, "For You silence (*dumiyah*, רמיה) is praise" (Psalm 65:2)? The medicine for everything is silence.
>
> When Rav Dimi came [from the Land of Israel], he said: In the West [i.e., the Land of Israel] they say: A word is worth a sela, silence two selas.

A note on the translation of Psalm 65:2 here. While it is here translated as "For you silence is praise," you will find it translated in the old (1917) Jewish Publication Society *Tanach* as "Praise waiteth for Thee, O God, in Zion" and in the new (1982) Jewish Publication Society Tanach as "Praise befits You in Zion, O God." The word *dumiyah* is used only four times in the entire *Tanach* (Psalms 22:3, 39:3, 62:2, and here, 65:2). In the other three occurrences it can be interpreted as "silence" or "rest," which is generally accomplished in silence.

We, with our limited powers of perception and expression, cannot ever praise the infinite God adequately. Therefore, we say those blessings provided for us by the tradition which we trust can express what we, as individuals, cannot. This *sugyah* is an echo of what we learned in tractate *Berachot* 33b.

> A certain [reader] went down in the presence of Rabbi Hanina and said, "God, the great, mighty, awesome, majestic, powerful, awful, strong, fearless, sure and honored." He waited till he had finished. When he had finished he said to him, "Have you finished off all the praise of your Master? What do I need all [these adjectives] for? Even with these three that we do say ["Great, mighty and awesome"], had not Moses our Teacher said them in the Torah (Deuteronomy 10:17) and had not the Men of the Great Assembly (Nehemiah 9:32) come and set them in the *Tefillah*, we would not have been able to say them, and you say all these [three] and still go on! It is as if a king of flesh and blood had a million denarii of gold, and someone praised him for some silver ones. Would it not be an insult to him?"

In these two *sugyot*, the rabbis touch on the basic paradox of prayer and Torah: The more deeply in touch with God we are, the less adequately words express our experiences of the Divine. Therefore, we use the words chosen by our ancestors — the *Shema*, the *Tefillah*, the *Hallel*, and the *Megillah* — to ritually express our relationship with God. The further along on our spiritual journey we progress, the more wordless the journey becomes. The rabbis hint at this when, after a discussion of how to praise God, they end by saying that silence is the best way.

Nonetheless, until we reach that elevated stage in our journeys, the words are very important. In fact, they are crucial, because they are the steps by which we rise in knowledge of God. Therefore the rabbis mandate that we take great care in their transmission.

> **GEMARA (18b):** The text [above states]: Rabbah bar Bar Hanah said in the name of Rabbi Johanan: It is forbidden to write one letter save from a manuscript.
>
> The following was cited in opposition to this by Rabbi Shimon ben Eleazar: It happened once that Rabbi Meir went to prolong the year in Asya and there was no *Megillah* there and he wrote one out by heart and read it! . . . And even so, Rabbi Meir could produce them correctly.
>
> Rav Hisda found Rav Hananel would write scrolls without a copy. He said to him: It would be fitting if the whole Torah would be written [by you] by heart, but thus have the Sages ruled: It is forbidden to write one letter save from a copy. . . .
>
> Abaye allowed the members of the household of Bar Havu (a *tefillin* vendor) to write *tefillin* and *mezuzot* without a manuscript. What authority did he follow? The following *Tanna*, as it has been taught: Rabbi Jeremiah says in the name of our Rabbi [Yehudah HaNasi]: *tefillin* and *mezuzot* may be written out without a manuscript, and do not require to be written upon ruled lines.
>
> The law is that *tefillin* do not require lines, but *mezuzot* do require lines and both may be written without a copy. What is the reason? They are well known by heart.

Many of the rabbis knew the entire *Tanach* and the *Mishnah* by heart. Therefore, when the reputation of the scribe was unimpeachable, such as Bar Havu's, or where the text was thought to be known by all, they did not require that a scribe copy the text from an existing scroll. However, in general they preferred that texts be copied from an existing scroll. When one is involved in the physical transmission of the tradition from one generation to the next, one cannot rely on memory, no matter how accurate.

The lines they refer to are called *shirtut* and are made by pressing a stylus into the parchment. Steinsaltz explains that the texts within *tefillin* do not require these lines because they are not read. In addition, the parchment used in the *tefillin* is often quite thin, since it must be tightly rolled to fit into the boxes of the *tefillin,* and the process of making the lines might tear the thin parchment. Torah scrolls, *Megillot, mezuzot,* and divorce decrees *(gittin)* all require these lines, as they are designed to be read.

However, no matter how important the physical presence of the text is, it is still only a vessel that helps us experience God's presence. God's presence is the true essence of the text, as those who have experienced it most intensely, Moses and Elijah, attest.

> **GEMARA (19b):** Rabbi Hiyya bar Abba also said in the name of Rabbi Johanan: Had there been in the cave in which Moses and Elijah stood a chink no bigger than the eye of a fine needle, they would not have been able to endure the light, as it says, "for man shall not see me and live" (Exodus 33:20).
>
> Rabbi Hiyya bar Abba also said in the name of Rabbi Johanan: What is the meaning of the verse, "And on them was written according to all the words which the Lord spoke with you in the mount" (Deuteronomy 9:10)? It teaches us that the Holy One, blessed be He, showed Moses the fine points of the Torah and the fine points of the Scribes, and the innovations which would be introduced by the Scribes; and what are these? The reading of the *Megillah.*

According to tradition, Moses and Elijah stood in the same cave when they each had their direct contact with God. It was in this cave that Elijah heard the still small voice (see 1 Kings 19:9–18) and in this cleft of rock that God shielded Moses from seeing the Divine Presence (Exodus 33:22). Directly seeing a small part of the light of God's presence was so overwhelming an experience that the rabbis believed that even Elijah and Moses could not stand its intensity. They would not have been able to stand the light, and so hid in this cave. Even these men had to have their experience of God mediated through words. God uses words for our benefit, not for God's own, to mediate between God's presence and our consciousness.

The second paragraph of this *sugyah* defines Torah as a process that does not *end* at the moment of contact with God, but rather *starts* there. Moses stood on the mount, and God unfolded before him the whole process by which innovations would develop in Judaism. In other words, innovations and change are built into the system. Thus, when changes are consistent with Moses' vision, we can be sure that they stand authentically in the chain of tradition. Even such an innovation as the reading of the *Megillah*, which Moses could not have known about unless he was granted a vision of it can be seen as consistent with earlier traditions. In this way, the rabbis can reconcile the fact that the reading of the *Megillah* was an innovation not ordained in the Torah with their belief that it was consistent with the chain of tradition they received.

### Midrash on Psalms, Psalm 29, #2*

Moses, upon being asked, "Whence do we know how many prayers we are to offer?" answered: "Mark how many times the Ineffable Name occurs in this Psalm." Told, "Eighteen times," Moses answered: "You must offer Eighteen Benedictions." Hence it is said, "The glory due unto His name," and hence also the preceding verse conjoins "glory and strength."

Asked, "Whence do we know where to begin?" Moses answered, "Mark the beginning of the Psalm: 'Ascribe unto the Lord, O ye sons of the mighty' (Psalm 29:1)—that is, 'the sons of Abraham, Isaac and Jacob'. So you must say in the first benediction: 'The God of Abraham, the God of Isaac, and the God of Jacob.'

"And as in the second occurrence of the Ineffable Name it is said, 'Ascribe unto the Lord glory and strength' (Psalm 29:1), so you must ascribe unto Him glory and strength with 'Blessed are You . . . who quickens the dead.'

"And as in the third occurrence of the Ineffable Name it is said, 'Ascribe unto the Lord the glory due unto His name' (Psalm 29:2), so you must bless Him with 'Blessed are You . . . the holy God.'

"Next, 'Worship the Lord in the beauty of holiness' (Psalm

---

*Translated by William G. Braude (New Haven, CT: Yale University Press, 1959), pp. 381–384.

29:2), that is, worship the Lord who gives knowledge to the holy, for 'The knowledge of the holy is understanding' (Proverbs 9:10)—calls for the benediction 'Blessed are You . . . gracious giver of knowledge.'

"Next, 'The voice of the Lord is upon the waters' (Psalm 29:3)—that is, upon repentance, which is likened to water in the verse, 'In repentance, they poured out their hearts before the Lord like water (1 Samuel 7:6)'—calls for the benediction 'Blessed are You . . . who delights in repentance.'

"Next, 'The Lord is upon the many waters' (Psalm 29:3)— that is 'You are a God . . . that pardons iniquity. . . . You will cast all their sins into the depths of the sea' (Micah 7:18–19)— calls for the benediction 'Blessed are You . . . who is gracious and does abundantly pardon.'

"Next, 'The voice of the Lord is powerful' (Psalm 29:4)— that is, 'I will redeem you with an outstretched arm' (Exodus 6:6), for God is described as 'Marching in the greatness of His strength' (Isaiah 63:1) in the age to come—calls for the benediction 'Blessed are You . . . the redeemer of Israel.'

"Next, 'The voice of the Lord is a glorious voice' (Psalm 29:4)—that is, in healing the sick, He restores to them the glory of health—calls for the benediction 'Blessed are You . . . who heals the sick of Your people Israel.'

"Next, 'The voice of the Lord breaks the cedars' (Psalm 29:5) calls for the benediction, 'Blessed are You . . . who blesses the years.' The men who raise prices and give small measure, and the rich men who live in plenty and appear strong as cedars—such men the Lord breaks to bits when He blesses His world by bringing low prices to it, thereby breaking the staff of wickedness. Hence, the verse calls for the benediction, 'Blessed are You . . . who blesses the years.'

"Next, 'The voice of the Lord breaks in pieces the cedars of Lebanon' (Psalm 29:5), that is, the Lord breaks in pieces the wicked nations of the earth that stand high as cedars, 'whose height is like the height of the cedars' (Amos 2:9), and He will gather the banished from the midst of the nations—calls for the benediction 'Blessed are You . . . who gathers the banished of Your people Israel.'

"Next, 'The voice of the Lord hews out flames of fire'

(Psalm 29:7)—that is, the judgments hewn out of the Lord's word are like flames of fire, for God says, 'Is not My word like as fire?' (Jeremiah 23:29), and also, 'By fire will the Lord execute judgment' (Isaiah 66:16)—calls for the benediction 'Blessed are You . . . who loves righteousness and judgment.'

"Next, 'The voice of the Lord shakes the wilderness (Psalm 29:8)'—that is, as the wilderness is barren, so wicked men are barren, so barren in good deeds that the Holy One blessed be He, shakes them to pieces—calls for the benediction 'Blessed are You . . . who breaks the enemies and humbles the proud.'

"Next, 'The Lord shakes the wilderness of Kadesh' (Psalm 29:8)—that is, the righteous are in an exile which resembles the wilderness of Kadesh where there was no water for the people, as Scripture relates, 'The people abode in Kadesh' (Numbers 20:1), where 'There was no water for the congregation' (Numbers 20:2), and where water returned only because of the merit of Moses and Aaron—calls for the benediction 'Blessed are You . . . the stay and trust of the righteous.'

"Next, 'The voice of the Lord brings forth hinds' (Psalm 29:9): Deliverers like hinds shall be born to Israel, as is said, 'My beloved is like a roe or a young hart' (Song of Songs 2:9); 'He makes my feet like hinds' feet' (2 Samuel 22:34); and 'How beautiful upon the mountains are the feet of him that brings good tidings' (Isaiah 52:7). 'The voice of the Lord . . . strips the forests bare' (Psalm 29:9): The Lord will strip the [hostile] nations of the earth who are like forests of their might, for it is said 'The Lord of hosts . . . will cut down the thickets of the forest with iron' (Isaiah 10:34). 'And in His Temple does every one speak of His glory (Psalm 29:9)': Once the Messiah comes and punishes the wicked nations of the earth, the Temple will be rebuilt forthwith. Hence the benediction 'Blessed are You . . . God of David who builds Jerusalem.' . . .

"Next, 'The Lord sits above the water-flood (Psalm 29:10)'—that is, when the Lord sat down [during the deluge] to judge the wicked, He hearkened to the prayers of those who came into Noah's ark, as is said, 'God remembered Noah, and every living thing . . . and the waters assuaged' (Genesis 8:1). Hence the benediction 'Blessed are You . . . who hearkens unto prayer.'

"Next, 'The Lord remains a king for ever' (Psalm 29:10) — that is, calmed by Noah's offering, the Lord had pity upon the earth, as is said, 'The Lord smelled the sweet savor; and . . . said . . . Not again will I curse the ground (Genesis 8:21)' — calls for the benediction 'Blessed are You . . . for You alone we worship in reverence.'

"And next, 'The Lord gives strength unto His people' (Psalm 29:11) — that is, gives the goodly strength of Torah, of which God said: 'I give you a good doctrine, forsake you not My law (Proverbs 4:2)' — calls for the benediction 'Blessed are You . . . whose name is All-good, and unto whom it is becoming to give thanks.'

"And finally, 'The Lord blesses His people with peace (Psalm 29:11)' calls for the benediction 'Blessed are You . . . who makes peace.' "

# 3

# The Text and the Synagogue

If we can liken the material in Chapter 1 to the intense experience of learning a piece of music and composing variations on its themes, and the material in Chapter 2 to singing that music and its variations for oneself, standing in one's living room as if in a concert, then the material in this chapter may be likened to singing that music to one's musical club. (The experience of singing at Carnegie Hall is covered in Chapter 4.) We have covered the experience of direct text study, then contact with the text in a ritual way. Now we move on to contact with the text in the realm of the Jewish community at prayer: the text's place in the synagogue. In order to explore this topic, the rabbis broaden their examination of text to include not just the *Megillah*, but the texts more often read in synagogue, the Torah and the portions of the Prophets read in the *Haftarah*.

> **MISHNAH (21a):** One who reads the *Megillah* [may do so either] standing or sitting. Whether one reads it or two read it [together], they [the congregation] have performed their obligation. In places where it is the custom to say a blessing [after the reading], it should be said, and where it is not the custom it need not be said.
>
> On Mondays and Thursdays and on Sabbath at *Minchah*, three read [from the Torah], neither more nor less, nor is a haftarah read from a Prophet. The one who reads first in the Torah and the one who reads last make [respectively] a blessing before reading and after.

On New Moons and the intermediate days of festivals four read, neither more nor less, and there is no Haftarah from the Prophets. The one who reads first and the one who reads last in the Torah make a blessing before and after.

This is the rule: Any day which has a *Musaf* [service] and is not a festival four read; on a festival five read; on the Day of Atonement six read; on Sabbath seven read. This number [of readers] may not be diminished but it may be added to, and a *Haftarah* is read from a Prophet.

The one who reads first and the one who reads last in the Torah make a blessing before and after [the reading].

Jewish practice regarding the Torah reading has not changed much since the days when this mishnah was formulated. Of course, now, when we have an *aliyah* to the Torah, we usually say the blessings over the reading that someone else, called the *Ba'al* (or *Ba'alat*) *Korei* (Master of Reading) performs, rather than reading from the Torah ourselves. Another change in Torah reading practice since the days of the *Mishnah* occurred in the way we say the blessings over the Torah reading. As the *mishnah* describes the practice, the first reader would say the opening blessing and read from the Torah, a second person would read from the Torah without reciting any blessings, and the last person would read and then say the closing blessing. The *Gemara* reports that this was changed so that each person who had an *aliyah*—an opportunity to read from and/or bless the Torah—said the blessings before and after the readings. This was done in order to avoid giving the impression to someone walking in late, that is, just when the persons between the first and last readers began to read, that the Torah was being read without a blessing. (It is noteworthy that late arrival at worship services was apparently in vogue then, as now!)

The rulings of the *Mishnah* regarding the number of *aliyot* we have on different days were decided using the following principle: the more signs of holiness the day has, the more *aliyot* will be said on it. Thus, a normal weekday with no other celebrations on it and the Afternoon Service *(Minchah)* on Shabbat will have three *aliyot*; the New Moon *(Rosh Chodesh)* and the intermediate days of the festivals (the days between the first and last days of Sukkot and Pesach) have four *aliyot;* on festivals we have five *aliyot;* on Yom Kippur we have six; on Shabbat, seven. Shabbat is considered the most honored of days. This is quite logical. Shabbat existed before there was a Jewish people, it is mentioned in the Ten Commandments, and it is in many ways the foundation of Jewish life. The Day of Atonement was established later, and while it is very important, it does not regulate Jewish life as much as the Sabbath does. (See the *Gemara* on this *mishnah,* below.)

The *Haftarah* is a selection from the Prophets (Joshua through the Latter Prophets) that either parallels the Torah portion in some way or is determined by the calendar or history. An example of the former category is the *Haftarah* for the Torah portion *Beshalach* (Exodus 13:17–17:16). That portion contains the Song at the Sea, and its *Haftarah* is also a song, the Song of Deborah (Judges 4:4–5:31). An example of the latter category are the special *Haftarot* we read between Tisha B'Av and Rosh HaShanah, the *Haftarot* of consolation, or the special *Haftarot* we read before Purim and Pesach. (See "The Four Portions" in the Glossary.)

The origin of the reading of the *Haftarah* is a matter of debate. Many believe that it was instituted during the reign of Antiochus Epiphanes, who ruled from 175–165 B.C.E. His persecution of the Jews eventually led to the Hasmonean revolt, the basis of Hanukkah. Torah study was forbidden at that time, so Jews may have read those portions from the Prophets that paralleled the Torah portions they *would* have read, had they been allowed to do so. According to this theory, when Torah reading was again permitted, Jews maintained the custom of reading a selection from the Prophets each week. Others theorize that the *Haftarah* reading may have been instituted to provide those who arrived at services late the opportunity to hear a selection from Scriptures on Shabbat.

The format of a blessing, followed by a reading from Scripture or other exalted activity, and then another blessing, is one we see throughout Jewish practice. Our meals are preceded and followed by blessings, as are whole sections of our liturgy. For example, before we recite the *Shema,* we say two blessings, and after we recite it, we say one or two blessings.

We recite blessings before and after the Torah and *Haftarah* readings and may do so with the *Megillah* reading, as well, as we shall see below.

We should note well the flexibility and respect for local custom that the rabbis show in this *mishnah*. We may read from the *Megillah* standing or sitting. One may read or many may read. If our synagogue has the custom of saying a blessing after the *Megillah* reading, then we may say the blessing. If our synagogue does not follow that custom, then we need not say this blessing after the reading. Not every question of Jewish practice had to be centrally decided upon; the system is endowed with flexibility and leaves us room for individual preference and expression.

The rabbis seemed ambivalent about many aspects of the Book of Esther. For example, the idea that we seem to be rejoicing almost vindictively at the downfall of an enemy seemed to trouble them. In the case of Hanukkah, the rabbis were able to shift the emphasis of the story from the military victory to a more spiritual celebration of rededication and purity. However, the story of Purim does not lend itself as easily to such reinterpretation. So the rabbis faced the issue head-on:

> **GEMARA (21b):** What blessing is said before the reading of the *Megillah?* Rav Shesheth from Katrazya happened once to be in the presence of Rav Ashi, and he made the blessings *Mikra, Nissim, Shehechiyanu.*
>
> What blessing is said after it [the reading of the *Megillah*]? "Blessed are You, O Lord our God, Ruler of the Universe, [the God] who *fought* our fight and *vindicated* our cause and *executed* our vengeance and *punished* our adversaries for us and *visited* retribution on all the enemies of our soul. Blessed are You, O Lord, who avenges Israel on all their enemies."
>
> Rava said: [The concluding words are], "The God who saves."
>
> Rav Papa said: Therefore let us say both: "Blessed are You, O Lord, who avenges Israel on all their enemies, the God who saves."

Clearly, the rabbis legitimate our happiness at God's avenging us. Rava proposes a different *chatimah*, the closing summation of the blessing—one that praises God's saving power rather than God's powerful vengeance. Rav Papa provides the characteristic answer to the question "Which prayer do we choose?"—"Both!" The rabbis are wrestling with their happiness at God's vengeance on our enemies and their sense that there is something somewhat improper about that happiness. They therefore allow us our happiness, but they hint that it is something we should outgrow in the way they finally formulate the blessing. At first, we may praise God's avenging power, but then we should learn to value God's saving power as well.

The rabbis do not deny basic human nature. When someone has hurt us badly, we do seek vengeance. There is no sense pretending that this is not so. They allow us these feelings and formulate blessings that help us consecrate and control them.

The five verbs italicized in the prayer above correspond to the five times Israel makes war with Amalek in the Scriptures (Exodus 17:8–16, Numbers 14:41–45, Judges 3:12–13, Judges 7:9–8:9, 1 Samuel 14:49–15:35). A similar *midrash* with which we may be more familiar is made on Exodus 6:6–7: "Therefore say to the children of Israel, I am the Lord, and I *will bring* you out from under the burdens of Egypt, and I *will deliver* you out of their bondage, and I *will redeem* you with an outstretched arm, and with great judgments. And I *will take* you to me for a people." Some authorities relate the four cups of wine drunk at a Passover *seder* to these four verbs of salvation. (In fact, now that you have a better understanding of the midrashic process, you will see that the *seder* is, in large part, an extended *midrash* on Deuteronomy 26:5–8.)

Perhaps the most familiar instance of this celebration of God's avenging power can be found at the end of the Passover *seder*, when we ask God,

"Pour out Your wrath upon those who do not know You and upon the governments which do not call upon Your name. For they have devoured Jacob and laid waste his dwelling place" (Psalm 79:6–7). "Pour out Your fury upon them, let the fierceness of Your anger overtake them" (Psalm 69:25). "Pursue them

in indignation and destroy them from under Your heavens"
(Lamentations 3:66).

Our relationship with God is an all-encompassing one. When
we are downtrodden and oppressed, when havoc has been
wreaked on us, we want justice, if not vengeance. When God
delivers that justice, we feel vindicated and glad. Remember
that it was the *angels* who were ordered not to rejoice when the
Egyptians drowned at the Red Sea, not the children of Israel.
To request *them* not to be happy as they saw their oppressors
crushed might have been too great an act of magnanimity to
ask.

    The blessings that precede the *Megillah* reading are less
problematic. The blessing for *Mikra* (reading) is the standard
blessing form: "Blessed are You, *Adonai* our God, Ruler of the
Universe, who hallows us with *mitzvot* . . ." followed by the
phrase ". . . and commanded us concerning the reading of the
*Megillah*." The blessing for *Nissim* is the same one we say on
Hanukkah: "Blessed are You, *Adonai* our God, Ruler of the
Universe, Who did miracles for our ancestors in those days at
this time." The *Shehechiyanyu*, "Blessed are You, Adonai our
God, Ruler of the Universe, who has kept us alive, and
sustained us and brought us to this time," is a prayer we say on
every holiday. On Purim, we praise God for text, for God's role
in history, and for God's role in our own lives.

    The *Gemara* comments on our mishnah, examining the
meaning behind the different number of *aliyot*.

    **GEMARA (21b):** "On Mondays and Thursdays and on Sab-
bath at *Minchah* three read." What do these three represent? Rav
Assi said: The Torah, the Prophets, and the Writings.
    Rava said: Priests, Levites, and lay Israelites.

Why do we have exactly three *aliyot* to the Torah on
Mondays, Thursdays, and Shabbat afternoon? Rav Assi relates
the *aliyot* to the three sections of the *Tanach*, while Rava relates
them to the three classes of Jews: Priests, Levites, and the rest
of the Jewish people. This is, in fact, the way Jews are still
called to the Torah today in traditional congregations. *Cohanim*,
those descended from priestly families, are called first, then

*Levi'im*, those descended from Levitical families, are called, and finally any Jew may be called for the remaining *aliyot*.

What is the basic disagreement between the views of the two rabbis? They differ on what is to be emphasized more in Judaism: the text or the people. Assi seems to say the former, Rava the latter, and while both views may be accepted, Rava's was the one that was put into practice. This order is even hinted at in the blessing for the Torah itself, which reads, "Blessed are You . . . who has chosen us from all the peoples, and given us the Torah." This blessing implies that if we had not existed as a people and been chosen to receive the Torah, it would not have been given, even though it would have existed. In other words, if we liken the Torah to a marriage contract between us and God, it would have quite a different meaning if God did not take us as a partner. It is when Torah binds us to God that it has the most meaning.

Another alternative explanation for these different categorizations could put an entirely different light on the topic. Rav Assi may have wanted to emphasize that all three sections of the *Tanach* should be studied. Rava may have wanted to relate the Torah reading to the groups of people who operated the Temple cult as a reminder of its primacy in Jewish life.

The reasoning behind the other various numbers of *aliyot* on different occasions is more obvious:

> **GEMARA (22b):** Come and hear: This the rule: any [holiday on which an extensive Torah reading would involve] a hindrance of the people [in their] work, as on a public fast and on the ninth of *Av*, three read, and where the people would not be hindered from their work, as on New Moons and the intermediate days of festivals, four read. . . .
>
> This is the rule: for every additional distinguishing mark an additional person reads. On the New Moon and the intermediate days of a festival, when there is an additional sacrifice, four read; on festivals, when [in addition] work is prohibited, five read; on the Day of Atonement when [in addition] there is a penalty of *kareit*, six read; on Sabbath when there is a penalty of stoning, seven read.

For every additional mark of holiness, we read an additional *aliyah*. On New Moons and intermediate days of a festival, we are permitted to work, in the sense that the restrictions against work associated with Shabbat, such as the prohibition against using fire, are not in force. However, these are half-holidays; days to take it easy. In American life we might liken these days to the day after Thanksgiving. It is not a holiday, but schools are closed and many people take off work. In addition, an extra sacrifice was offered while the Temple stood, so an extra *aliyah* is added to the reading for these "half-holidays." On Festivals, such as Passover or Shavuot, work is prohibited, which is an extra sign of holiness, so an *aliyah* is added for that reason. Violations of Yom Kippur are punished by *kareit*, interpreted by the rabbis to mean punishment of premature death brought by God. Finally, violations of Shabbat are punished by death by stoning, the most severe punishment in Jewish law.

Now that the rabbis have determined how many persons may read Torah in a community on any given day, they begin to examine *who* may read. Specifically, may women read the Torah at services, or may they not? One might think that they are not obligated to do so, since it is a positive, time-bound commandment, from which women are exempt. However, the rabbis disqualify women for a different reason, *kevod hatsibbur*, "respect for the congregation":

> **GEMARA (23a):** Our Rabbis taught: All are qualified to be among the seven [who read], even a minor and even a woman. However, the Sages said that a woman should not read in the Torah out of respect for the congregation [*kevod hatsibbur*].

Of the seven times the phrase *kevod hatsibbur* is mentioned in the Talmud, three of them occur in this tractate. Let us examine the other cases to which this term is applied before we come to any conclusions about it and its use here. All of the rules that are justified by this rationale of *kevod hatsibbur* seem to concern the smooth running of the synagogue.

> **Yoma (70a):** R. Huna the son of R. Joshua said in the name of R. Sheshet: Because it is not proper to roll up a scroll of the Law before the community because of *"kevod hatsibbur,"* respect for the congregation.

One does not take the time, while the congregation sits, to roll the Torah from one place to another far distant (for example, when one passage in Exodus and another in Deuteronomy are read on the same day, as they are on *Shabbat Zachor* [see Glossary, "The Four Portions"]). Imagine sitting in synagogue waiting for twenty minutes as the Torah was laboriously rolled. You would lose your concentration and might be tempted to leave the service altogether, which certainly does not redound to the honor of the congregation.

> **Sotah (39b):** The Precentor is not permitted to strip the ark bare in the presence of the congregation because of respect for the congregation.

Similarly, in the days when the ark was dismantled and put away, one waited until after services were over to do this, rather than interrupt the flow of the service with this commotion. Again, imagine you were at services and, as soon as the Torah reading was over, but before the service was over, the janitor came in and started to clean up, putting away the books and cloths used in the Torah reading. It would definitely cause a stir in the congregation and distract your attention from the service.

> **Sotah (40a):** The Rabbis said: It is derived from the regulation that the *kohanim* are not permitted to ascend the platform wearing their shoes. This is one of the ten ordinances which Rabbi Johanan ben Zakkai instituted. What was the reason? Was it not out of respect for the congregation? Rav Ashi said: No; [the reason] there was lest the shoelace become untied and he proceeds to retie it, and people will say, "He is the son of a divorcee or a *chalutsah*."

When a Cohen, a member of the priestly family, was called to the *bimah*, the dais, to bless the people with the Priestly Benediction (Numbers 6:24–26), the congregation wanted to feel confident that this was a fit descendant of a priestly family. A priest who blesses the public may not be the son of a divorced woman or a woman whose husband had died childless and who was subsequently released from the obligation to marry her husband's brother, a *chalutsah*. Anything that would cast doubt on the *Cohen*'s fitness to bless the people had to be obviated in order that the service run smoothly. His pausing on his way to the *bimah* to fix his shoe might be interpreted as a reluctance to take the honor. In turn, this might lead to suspicions that he was reluctant to take the honor because he was unfit to do so.

> **Gittin (60a):** Rabbah and R. Joseph both concurred in ruling that separate *humashin* [separate scrolls of each book of the Torah] should not be read from out of respect for the congregation.

In ancient times both the entire Torah and the five individual books of the Torah were written in scrolls. To read from one of the smaller scrolls just would not seem right – not a correct Torah reading in its full honor and ceremony. Therefore, the sages mandate that each congregation should have a complete Torah scroll. Today, imagine your congregation reading the Torah portion out of a Pentateuch book rather than the scroll. It would not have the same effect as reading out of the scroll itself.

Finally, certain norms of acceptable communal behavior must be observed at worship services, such as norms of dress:

> *(Megillah)* **GEMARA (24b):** "A person in rags may . . . not read in the Torah nor pass before the ark." Ulla bar Rav enquired of Abaye: Is a child in rags allowed to read in the Torah? He replied: You might as well ask about a naked one. Why is one without any clothes not allowed? Out of respect for the congregation. So here, [he is not allowed] out of respect for the congregation.

First let us examine the simple meaning of this *sugyah*. A person in rags might risk exposing himself in a way that could be taken as sexual, and this seems a clear flaunting of the communal norms. Ulla bar Rav asks about a child since he may assume that a child, having no developed sexual characteristics, might not have a problem participating in the service.

However, it becomes clear that even aside from the risk of exposing oneself sexually there appear to be certain acceptable norms of dress for synagogue services.

This *sugyah* may make us feel uncomfortable until we think about it in a modern context. Imagine you are attending High Holiday services when a person approaches the *bimah* to have an *aliyah*. Now imagine this person is wearing a jogging outfit or a bathing suit. Would you really be concentrating on the Torah reading as this person had an *aliyah*? Or would you be more likely to look at the individual and feel dismayed at the inappropriate dress? Of course, issues regarding the poor and their dress are more troubling. Are the poor truly to be denied the chance to approach the Torah because they are dressed in rags? The obvious answer is that we should work to prevent this situation by providing them with decent clothing.

When viewed against this background, it appears that the reason women were not called to the Torah was not because they were inherently unqualified to read or bless it, but because doing so would violate the norms of their community. In the days of the Talmud, decorum required that a certain set of rules be followed regarding the text read, the number of allowable interruptions in the flow of the service, and a standard of "presentable" dress. Women reading from the Torah evidently did not conform to this sense of decorum. The rabbis may have been concerned that they would improperly expose themselves as they came to the Torah or that their voice or appearance would be sexually stimulating in an inappropriate way.

The idea of women's participation in worship services today can inflame people's passions. It may help each community in determining its own practices to understand the concept of *kevod hatsibbur* in the Talmud and examine whether their ideas of communal decorum correspond to the Talmud's. We should note once more that women were excluded from participating in the Torah service not because they were inherently unqualified, but because of communal norms. (We might also note that many Jewish communal norms have changed since the time of the Talmud. For example, bigamy was allowed in the rabbis' day but has since been banned because of societal norms.)

The rabbis are concerned not just with the honor of the congregation, but with the honor of the Jewish people and the Torah itself. Even though we think of the rabbis as unambivalently urging the study of Torah, they actually temper this attitude when such study would damage the honor of the Torah or the Jewish people. Note that in our next *sugyah* the rabbis are concerned with what can be read and translated at worship services. Their concern is for the honor due the Torah and the Jewish people in the sphere of the synagogue, the topic of this chapter.

> **MISHNAH (25a):** The incident of Reuben (Genesis 35:22) is read in synagogue but not translated.
>
> The story of Tamar (Genesis 38) is read and translated.
>
> The first account of the incident of the golden calf (Exodus 32:1–20) is both read and translated, the second (Exodus 32:21–25) is read but not translated.
>
> The blessing of the priests (Numbers 6:24–27) and the stories of David (2 Samuel 11:2–17) and Amnon (2 Samuel 13:1–22) are read but not translated.
>
> The portion of the Chariot (Ezekiel 1 and 10) is not read as a *Haftarah*, but Rabbi Judah permits this. Rabbi Eleazar says: The portion "make known to Jerusalem" (Ezekiel 16) is not read as a *Haftarah*.

This *sugyah* lists those sections of the *Tanach* that are simply read without being translated for the congregation and those sections that are read and translated. Ancient synagogues did not provide each worshiper with a Pentateuch from which to follow the weekly Torah reading. Therefore, the texts were read and then translated for the benefit of the non-Hebrew speakers in the congregation.

Let us take each of these portions in turn and see what common thread connects them.

1. **Genesis 35:22 reads,** "And it came to pass, when Israel dwelt in that land, that Reuben went and lay with Bilha his father's concubine, and Israel heard of it." This is read but not translated so as not to bring shame on the Jewish people, for it portrays Reuben as an adulterer and one who does not have

sufficient respect for his father. (Sleeping with one's father's concubine was taken as a sign of insolence.)

2. **The story of Tamar and Judah** (Genesis 38:1–30) is read and translated, even though it involves an improper sexual liaison. Tamar marries Judah's two sons, Er and Onan, who both die because they apparently practice some kind of sexual immorality. Tamar, having no children, is entitled to marry Judah's third son, Shela, but Judah denies her this, fearing that this son, too, shall die. Therefore, Tamar is reduced to dressing as a harlot and tricking Judah into sleeping with her. She becomes pregnant from this union with the twins Perets and Zerach. Perets is the ancestor of King David (Ruth 4:18–22), and the desire to publicly mark the beginning of this lineage outweighs the shame of the improper sexual relations enough to translate the story. Then, too, the union in this story, while not exactly proper, does stem from a just cause and results in a great family within the Jewish people.

3. **The rabbis draw a distinction** between the two reported versions of the golden calf story. The first is Exodus 32:1–20 and the second is Exodus 32:21–25. According to Rashi, the crux of the problem with this second telling of the golden calf story, in which Aaron is trying to explain to Moses what has happened, is the phrase, "They broke it [the gold] off and gave it to me: then I threw it into the fire, and there came out this calf" (Exodus 32:24). Lest someone hear this last phrase and think that the idol was actually animated or was magically formed by some spirit or through its own power, this verse is not translated.

4. **The *Gemara* on this *mishnah*** comments that the Priestly Blessing is not translated because it contains the phrase "May He lift up His countenance upon you" (Numbers 6:26). This verb can be interpreted to imply that God "plays favorites" for Israel, and so it is not translated in order to avoid giving this impression to non-Jews who do not understand Hebrew.

Obviously, the rabbis must have felt ambivalent on this point, because Israel's election by God is emphasized in many ways throughout Judaism. We were chosen to receive the

Torah. We were favored by God's championship of our causes before Pharaoh, Haman, and countless other enemies. The rabbis harmonize these two concepts, that God does not show favoritism and that Jews *are* shown special favor, by relating the honor God shows the Jews to their performance of *mitzvot, not* to a whim on God's part. The sages are careful to maintain that God's system is just and understandable, unlike pagan religious systems in which the deities were capricious.

This issue is addressed directly in tractate *Berachot,* where God explains that Jews are shown Divine favor because of their particular observance of the *mitzvot:*

> **Berachot, Gemara 20b:** The ministering angels said before the Holy One, blessed be He: Sovereign of the Universe, it is written in Your Torah, "Who regards not persons [literally: who lifts not up the countenance] nor takes reward" (Deuteronomy 10:17), and do You not regard the person of Israel, as it is written, "The Lord lift up His countenance upon You" (Numbers 6:26)? He replied to them: And shall I not lift up My countenance for Israel, seeing that I wrote for them in the Torah, "And you shall eat and be satisfied and bless the Lord your God" (Deuteronomy 8:10), and they are particular [to say grace] if the quantity is but an olive or an egg.

With this *sugyah* from *Berachot,* the rabbis are affirming that Jews are, in fact, favored by God, but only because of our performance of *mitzvot.* This may be difficult for modern readers to accept. Some may be uncomfortable with the concept that Jews are favored more than anyone else before God. However, in this, as in many areas, the rabbis are able to see both sides of a coin at once. In some ways, non-Jews are just as, if not more, favored than Jews. All a non-Jew must do to achieve redemption is observe the seven Noachide commandments (prohibitions against idolatry, blasphemy, bloodshed, sexual sins, theft, and eating from a living animal, as well as the commandment to establish a legal system), while Jews must observe all the *mitzvot* to achieve that same redemption. Of course, whether you see yourself as favored or penalized depends on how you regard the *mitzvot:* as a burden to be borne or a vehicle for redemption to be embraced. Jews and non-Jews can each be seen to be favored in their own way.

5. **The story of David's infidelity** with Bathsheba and his indirectly causing the death of her husband, Uriah, are read but not translated, for obvious reasons. This story casts David in a shameful light. The story of David's son, Amnon's, rape of his half-sister Tamar is not translated for the same reason.

6. **The portions of the Chariot** are a mystic vision in Ezekiel. In tractate *Hagigah* (11a), this portion is included in a list of topics prohibited for study unless one is "a sage and understands of his own knowledge." Otherwise one might misinterpret these passages. Since most members of the congregation are not sages, we do not read these passages as a *Haftarah*. The sixteenth chapter of Ezekiel tells in detailed fashion how the Jews partook in idolatry and of God's anger with them. Therefore it is not read as a *Haftarah* in order to avoid making the congregation feel too ashamed.

The *Gemara* that follows this *mishnah* addresses the same issue: what portions of the Tanach are simply read, and which are read and translated in the synagogue? However, if we read the *Gemara* carefully, we will note that it is not commenting on the *mishnah* above it. Rather, it is commenting on a *tosefta* that covers the same material.

Our *mishnah* contained one list of scriptural passages and the rules regarding their reading and translation. The *tosefta* quoted in the Gemara provides a longer list of what is read and translated. Then it gives a list different from that of our *mishnah's* of what is read and *not* translated.

**GEMARA (25a):** Our rabbis taught: [Some portions of Scripture] are both read and translated, some are read but not translated, and some are neither read nor translated.

The following are both read and translated: (Mnemonic: BLT EKN NSHPH [*Bereishit, Lot, Tamar, Egel, Kelalot, Onshin, Amnon, Absalom, Pilegesh, Hoda*]). The account of the creation is both read and translated. Certainly! You might think that [through hearing it] people are led to inquire what is above and what is below (25b), and what is before and what is after. Therefore we are told [that this is not so].

The story of Lot and his two daughters is both read and translated. Certainly! You might think that [we should forbear] out of respect for Abraham. Therefore we are told [that this is not so].

The story of Tamar and Judah is both read and translated. Certainly! We might think that [we should forbear] out of respect for Judah. Therefore we are told [that this is not so]; [the passage] really redounds to his credit, because [it records that] he confessed.

The first account of the making of the Calf is both read and translated. Certainly! You might think that [we should forbear] out of respect for Israel. Therefore we are told [that this is not so]; on the contrary, it is agreeable to them, because it was followed by atonement.

The curses and blessings (Leviticus 26 and Deuteronomy 27) are both read and translated. Certainly! You might think [that we should forbear] lest the congregation should become disheartened; therefore we are told [that this is no objection].

Warnings and penalties are both read and translated. Certainly! You might think that [we should forbear] for fear that they may come to keep the commandments out of fear; therefore we are told [that this is no objection].

The story of Amnon and Tamar is both read and translated. Certainly! You might think that [we should forbear] out of respect for David. Therefore we are told [that this is no objection].

The story of the concubine in Gibea (Judges 19, 20) is both read and translated. Certainly! You might think [that we should forbear] out of respect for Benjamin. Therefore, we are told [that this is no objection].

The passage commencing "Make known to Jerusalem her abominations" is both read and translated. Certainly! This is stated to exclude the view of Rabbi Eleazar [who forbid it], as it has been taught: On one occasion a man read in the presence of Rabbi Eleazar, "Make known to Jerusalem her abominations." He said to him, "Before you investigate the abominations of Jerusalem, go and investigate the abominations of your own mother." Inquiries were made about him, and he was found to be illegitimate.

(Mnemonic: REBDN). [*Reuben, Egel, Berachah, David, Amnon*]. The incident of Reuben is read but not translated. It is a story that Rabbi Hanina ben Gamaliel went to Kavul, and the reader of the congregation read, "And it came to pass when Israel abode" (Genesis 35:22), and he said to the translator, "Stop. Translate only the latter part of the verse," and the sages commended his action.

The second account of the Calf is read but not translated. What is the second account of the Calf? – From "And Moses said" up to "and Moses saw" (Exodus 32:21–25). It has been taught, Rabbi Shimon ben Elazar says: A person should always be careful in wording his answers, because on the ground of the answer which Aaron made to Moses the unbelievers (i.e., *minim*) were able to deny [God], as it says, "And I cast it into the fire and this calf came out."

The priestly blessing is read but not translated. What is the reason? Because it contains the words, "May He lift up."

The accounts of David and Amnon are neither read nor translated. But you [just] said that the story of Amnon and Tamar is both read and translated? There is no contradiction; the former statement refers to where it says "Amnon son of David" [the first verse], and the latter to where it says "Amnon" simply.

Let us summarize the differences between the *mishnah* and the *Gemara* (and the *tosefta* quoted in it) before we continue our discussion.

| Story | Mishnah | Gemara |
|---|---|---|
| Genesis | not mentioned | read/translated |
| Lot and daughters | not mentioned | read/translated |
| Reuben | read/not translated | read/not translated |
| Tamar | read/translated | read/translated |
| Curses and Penalties | not mentioned | read/translated |
| Golden Calf (1st) | read/translated | not mentioned |
| Golden Calf (2nd) | read/not translated | read/not translated |
| Priestly blessing | read/not translated | read/not translated |
| Pilegesh | not mentioned | read/translated |
| David | read/not translated | not read/not translated |
| Amnon | read/not translated | read/translated (*and* not read/not translated) |
| Chariot | not read | not mentioned |
| "Make known to Jerusalem" | not read | read and translated |

First, let us examine the passages mentioned in the *Gemara* that are not cited in the mishnah.

The story of creation (Genesis 1:1) is read, even though it might cause the congregation to speculate on metaphysical questions of what came before God started creating the world. For example, they might ask, "Where did the *tohu* and *vohu*, the void, come from?" or "Where did God come from?" The rabbis did not want us to inquire as to what came before the Creation as described in Genesis. They explain that the Torah starts with the letter *bet* (ב) because it is closed above, below, and behind and opens only in the direction of the Torah text to indicate that we should not look above, behind, or below that letter for explanations of the world's genesis.

The story of Lot and his daughters (Genesis 19:30–38), in which the daughters intoxicate their father and sleep with him and become pregnant, aside from being a tale of sexual immorality, casts a negative light on Abraham, the first Jew. Lot was his brother's son, and Abraham's charge. Nevertheless, the story is read and translated, perhaps because it does not directly shame Abraham.

The rabbis worried that the lengthy list of curses in Leviticus 26 might cause the congregation to despair. Rashi seems to interpret the rabbis' concern about the blessings and curses in Deuteronomy 27 and 28 as leading the people to do the *mitzvot* for the wrong reasons. The people might do the *mitzvot* out of fear of punishment and desire for reward, when they should be done out of love and respect for God. However, the rabbis rule that these sections are read and translated as a fair way of letting the public know what the consequences of their actions will be.

The story of the concubine is set in Gibea (Judges 19, 20), which belonged to the tribe of Benjamin. A man and his concubine were traveling and were spending the night in Gibea when the people of the town demanded that the man come out so that they could sexually assault him. Instead, the concubine was sent out and was raped by the local men and died from the experience. When news of the crime was spread about, the Benjaminites refused to surrender the guilty parties and a bloody battle ensued. Obviously, this story casts shame on the tribe of Benjamin.

All of the sections of the Torah and Prophets listed in the mishnah and the Gemara raise concerns about the honor of the Jewish people and especially its royal, messianic, Davidic line. The rabbis even go so far as to say that when, in the story of Amnon's rape of Tamar, Amnon is referred to as David's son, the story is neither read nor translated. Where Amnon is not so named and does not directly cast aspersions on David's name, the story is read and translated.

Just as the *sugyah* regarding the translations into Greek in Chapter 1 (9a) showed us what troubled the rabbis in the text, this *sugyah* shows us what they considered to be deleterious to the honor of a Jewish congregation. (Interestingly, Genesis 1:1 is the only verse the two lists have in common.) The list in Chapter 1 dealt with more theological issues and *God's* honor, while this list concentrates more on the honor of the Jewish people. Again, we see the interplay of honor, text, and people at work. Here the honor of the people is uppermost in the rabbis' minds. In Chapter 1, it was God's honor, and thus the honor due the text itself, that was preeminent for them. The placement of these two *sugyot* in these two chapters underscores the underlying structure of the tractate. If they had wanted to put all the *sugyot* regarding translations in one chapter, they would have put these two together. Rather, they cite them in these two chapters because they dovetail with the themes of those chapters.

In exploring the roles honor and text play in the synagogue, the rabbis make it clear that one need not be a Torah scholar to derive benefit from Torah study personally as well as make a contribution to the community. Everyone can participate in and benefit from the honor Torah study brings individuals and communities.

**GEMARA (24b):** "A blind person may repeat the blessings before the *Shema* and translate. Rabbi Judah says: One who has never seen the light from his birth may not recite the blessings before the *Shema*."

It has been taught: They said to Rabbi Judah: Many have discerned sufficiently [with their mind's eye] to expound the Chariot and yet they never saw it? [What says] Rabbi Judah [to this]? There [he can reply], all depends on the discernment of the heart and the expounder by concentrating his mind can know [about the chariot], but here one reads for the benefit which he derives therefrom, and this one [i.e., a blind person] derives no benefit [from light].

The rabbis, however, hold that he does derive a benefit, for the reason given by Rabbi Jose, as it has been taught: Rabbi Jose said: All my days I was perplexed by this verse, "And you shall grope at noonday as the blind gropes in darkness" (Deuteronomy 28:29). Now what difference does it make to a blind man whether it is dark or light? [I did not find the answer to this question] until the following incident occurred.

One time, I was walking on a pitch black night when I saw a blind man walking in the road with a torch in his hand. I said to him, "My son, why do you carry this torch?" He said to me, "As long as I have this torch in my hand, people see me and save me from the holes and the thorns and the briars."

This story may be understood as a simple halachic decision: a blind person benefits from light even though he or she does not see it, and so can say the blessing for light that precedes the *Shema*. However, it is also possible to interpret this story as a parable in the following way. The torch in the story is the Torah. The blind person is the person who learns Torah but does not understand what he or she has learned. The light of Torah that you internalize protects you and sheds light on others, even when you don't fully sense its light. If you learn Torah and honor it (hold it high), you become a light to others, and those others, guided by that light, guide you when you are blind.

When we are granted a vision of or from God, we are not literally "seeing." There are many ways of internalizing light: vision may be the most obvious, but not the most potent, way. Just so, using our intellect may be the most obvious way to learn Torah, but it is certainly not the only, and maybe not even the best, way. We can treasure it by reading it, singing it, memorizing it, studying it, and letting it affect our lives. All these kinds of learning lend honor to the individuals who perform them and to the communities in which they reside.

# 4

# The Text and the World

In our ever-broadening circles of honor, we reach the widest sphere of influence of the text, and the honor it brings, in our lives. We began with our direct relationship to the text, moved next to encountering the text as prayer, then to the text in the synagogue, and now the Talmud examines how text and honor function in the world at large.

In the first *sugyah* of this chapter, we see this interaction played out in one of its most basic spheres: the intersection of the realm of the holy, the synagogue and the holy items within it, and the realm of commerce.

> **MISHNAH (25b):** If the townspeople sell the town square, they may buy with the proceeds a synagogue;
>
> [if they sell] a synagogue, they may buy [with the proceeds] an ark;
>
> [if they sell] an ark they may buy wrappings [for scrolls];
>
> [if they sell] wrappings (26a) they may buy books;
>
> [if they sell] books they may buy a [*Sefer*] *Torah*.
>
> But if they sold a [*Sefer*] *Torah* they may not buy [with the proceeds] books;
>
> if [they sell] books they may not buy wrappings;
>
> if [they sell] wrappings they may not buy an ark;
>
> if [they sell] an ark they may not buy a synagogue;
>
> if [they sell] a synagogue they may not buy a town square.
>
> The same applies to any money left over.

**GEMARA (26b):** Our rabbis taught: Accessories of a *mitzvah* may be thrown away. Accessories of holiness are stored away.

The following are accessories of a *mitzvah:* a *sukkah,* a *lulav,* a *shofar,* fringes.

The following are accessories of holiness: sacks [for keeping scrolls] of the Scripture in, *tefillin* and *mezuzot,* a case for a *Sefer Torah,* and a case for *tefillin* and *tefillin* straps.

The general principle expressed in this *sugyah* is one best learned in relation to the Hannukah candles: whenever possible, we raise something's level of holiness rather than diminish it (*Shabbat* 21b). In the case of the Hanukkah candles, this means we start with one and work our way up to eight, even though it would make just as much, or more, sense to start with eight and work our way down to one candle on the last day. For example, when the Tabernacle was dedicated, thirteen bullocks were sacrificed the first day, twelve on the second, and so on (Numbers 29:12ff.). Since Hanukkah shares some characteristics with that original dedication ceremony, it would be logical to have the candles correspond to the diminishing number of bullocks offered during the dedication. However, a principle of greater importance is the idea that we raise the level of holiness in things as much as possible, rather than lower it.

In this *mishnah,* the rabbis' rank ordering of the holiness in certain items is clearly displayed. As items become ever more closely related to the Torah scroll, greater holiness and honor accrue to them. The principle used to determine "what is most holy?" here is, "the closer to the Torah it is, the holier it is." It is almost as if they are "zeroing in" on the Torah scroll in their list in this mishnah. There are very few things holy enough to purchase with money made from the sale of a Torah scroll, as we will see below.

The *Gemara* draws a different distinction. It uses an extreme example to shed light on the question of what kind of honor is shown different ritual items. Everyone would agree that a Torah scroll, a set of *tefillin,* or a *mezuzah* are holy objects when they are whole and fit for use. But what honor is due such items when they are worn out? It is similar to asking what honor is due a person once they have died. Just as the rabbis are scrupulous to honor the dead, so they demand appropriate honor be shown holy items whose functional life is over. In fact, Jewish law mandates that any writing that contains God's name, even a business letter that mentions God's name in passing, be appropriately disposed of. Such a document is not thrown in the garbage or burned, but is carefully stored away. Places where such documents are stored away are called *genizot* (*genizah*, singular), literally, "storing away places."

The rabbis draw a distinction between accessories of *mitzvot* and accessories of holiness. Accessories of *mitzvot*, which may be thrown away, help one perform a *mitzvah*, but it is the *mitzvah* which is holy, not the object. So it is the *sitting* in the *sukkah*, the *waving* of the *lulav*, the *hearing* of the *shofar*, and the *wearing* of the *tsitsit* (the fringes), that is holy, not the objects themselves. When these items no longer enable us to perform *mitzvot*, they cease to command honor. However, those items that attach to the physical words of Torah maintain their holiness even after they have ceased to be useful. These objects have a holiness intrinsic in themselves. They must be stored away, rather than thrown out.

One last note on this first *mishnah* in Chapter 4: the structure outlined in this *mishnah* is reflected in the organization of the material in the chapter as a whole. Just as, throughout this tractate, we have moved in ever-widening circles of holiness, so in this chapter we will chart the effect of holiness and honor in the world at large, beginning again with the core, Torah, then moving to the accoutrements of holiness, then to the synagogue building, and then to the outside world, until the rabbis examine the impact of Torah and God's honor even in the furthest exile from the Land of Israel.

The rabbis devise a system that beautifully connects the honor due the Torah with the honor due each person as a creature created in God's image. The venue in which they expound this system is the proper storing away of accessories of holiness.

**GEMARA (26b):** Mar Zutra said: Wrappings of books [scrolls] which are worn out may be made into shrouds for a *meit* *mitzvah* (a dead person who has no one to bury him or her), and this constitutes their storing away.

Rava also said: A *Sefer Torah* which is worn out may be buried by the side of a *talmid hacham* [a student of a sage], and also by one who [only] repeats *halachot*.

First let us examine the simple meaning of these texts before we look at their underlying significance. The system the rabbis outline above recognizes that inanimate objects can become emotionally and spiritually charged through use and devotion. For example, one need only look at a dirty, bedraggled doll or blanket held tightly in a child's hand to know how much love has been showered on it. Cloths that were wrapped around holy books or Torah scrolls have a high level of holiness, almost as if they were a part of the holiness of the book itself.

Energy from actions, whether good or bad, is created and sustained throughout the systems that connect Jews to one another and to God. The energy invested in a Torah cover that is lovingly and respectfully touched and prayed over for years is not allowed to simply dissipate. When the time has come, these cloths are used for yet another *mitzvah:* burying a person who has no mourners.

For the rabbis, there could be no purer form of honor than the honor shown a *meit mitzvah.* A *meit mitzvah,* literally, a dead one [whose care is] commanded, is someone who has died and has no one to perform the last rites of purification and burial for him or her. It then becomes the community's responsibility to give this person a proper burial. Helping to bury the dead is one of the highest forms of showing honor in Judaism, for it is one of the few acts of charity that we know cannot be repaid by the person upon whom it is bestowed, and thus can have no aspect of self-interest to it. Note, too, that honor accrues to the *meit mitzvah* not because of anything intrinsic in him or her, but because of the honor inherently due any human being.

There is a hierarchy within this concept of a continuous flow of "*mitzvah* energy." Less holy items, such as wrappings for scrolls, are used to make the shroud of a *meit mitzvah.* The scroll itself is buried with a sage. The rabbis regard the Torah as equivalent to a person—and not just any person, but an especially honored one, at that. Here we see the rabbis' hierarchy regarding people come into play as well. To merit burial with a Torah scroll, one need not be the greatest sage that ever lived. Rather, one need only be the student of a sage, even if all one could do was recite the *mishnah* without interpreting it. Such a person who had internalized a great deal of text merits the honor of being buried with a Torah scroll. Holiness belongs with holiness of an equal magnitude.

It is told that during the Holocaust, five pious Jews decided that they would each learn one of the five books of the Torah by heart so that, even should the scrolls be taken from them, the words of Torah would not be lost. When Simchat Torah, the holiday of the Rejoicing of the Torah came, the community had no scrolls to lift up and dance with, so they lifted up these pious Jews instead and paraded them around in joy. A book can be on pages, but it can also be in people.

This equation of a Torah scroll to a person is seen clearly in our next *sugyah* as well.

> **GEMARA (27a):** Come and hear what Rabbi Johanan said in the name of Rabbi Meir: One does not sell a *Sefer Torah* except to study Torah or acquire a wife. . . .
>
> Our rabbis taught: A person should not sell a *Sefer Torah* even though he does not need it. Rabban Simeon ben Gamaliel went further and said: Even if a person has nothing to eat and he sells a *Sefer Torah* or his daughter, he will never see a sign of blessing [from that money].

The honor and love we bear a Torah scroll is equivalent to the love we have for a person, even one as close as a spouse or a child. We may sell a *Sefer Torah* in order to save and perpetuate life: to betroth a wife, to provide the means to study Torah (the rabbis obviously believed Torah study was equivalent to life), to save a terminally ill or starving person, or to redeem a captive. Torah without people to study it still has worth. However, the Torah's honor is diminished if it is not studied. However, the rabbis were ambivalent about selling a Torah. While they permitted us to sell them in dire circumstances, they preferred that we not do so, for it is likened to selling a child to pay the bills. Such a practice may sound shocking but, in fact, people in ancient days were sometimes forced to sell *themselves* into slavery to raise the money to pay their taxes.

The devotion of people is part of what makes a thing holy, and the more people that shower an object with devotion, the more holy it becomes.

> **MISHNAH (27b):** We do not sell [a holy thing] of the public to an individual because it lowers it in holiness. These are the words of Rabbi Meir.
>
> They said to him: If so, [then it could] not be sold from a big city to a small one.

> **GEMARA:** That was a sound objection raised by the rabbis against Rabbi Meir, [was it not]? What says Rabbi Meir to this? [To sell] from a large town to a small one [is unobjectionable], because if it was holy to begin with, it is still holy now. But if it passes from a community to an individual, there is no holiness left. [And what is the reply of] the rabbis [to this]? If that raises a scruple [in this case], in the other case also it raised a scruple, because "in the multitude of people is the king's glory" (Proverbs 14:28).

What is the "holy thing" the rabbis are speaking of? The Soncino translation of the Babylonian Talmud suggests that it is a synagogue, while the Jerusalem Talmud (3:2–3) suggests that a *Sefer Torah* may be referred to. (Steinsaltz quotes both opinions in his commentary.) This latter suggestion would make more practical sense, since it might be difficult to sell an entire synagogue to another city, while a Torah scroll could be more easily sold. Note again that we are dealing with the proper treatment of honor in the world at large: the selling of a Torah scroll between communities.

As we have seen, a *Sefer Torah* is considered equivalent to a person in many respects, and each congregation develops a relationship to its Torah scrolls. Many a *Sefer Torah*'s story of survival is known to the congregation that holds it. Once a community has developed a certain relationship with a *Sefer*

*Torah,* it would be akin to selling away one of its children to sell it to another community.

The *Gemara,* in its comment, seeks to determine where the truly crucial difference lies: Is it between a large community and a small one, or between a small community and an individual? Instead of making a clear decision, they place the issue on a continuum: The more people exposed to any given Torah, the better, for God's honor is increased when many people study Torah. The proof text from Proverbs seems to say that God is glorified by large gatherings of people, and indeed, such large congregations have a special spiritual power. While the rabbis maintain this view here, in other places in the Talmud they maintain that the number of worshipers after a *minyan* has been established is not relevant (e.g., *Berachot* 49b). Both venues for prayer have their place. One can achieve a special intensity of prayer in a very large congregation and an equally special, but different, intensity of prayer in a small congregation. We can understand the rabbis' system if we think of where the Mona Lisa should be properly stored. Should it be in a large museum where throngs of people have easy access to it? Should it be in a small, out-of-the-way museum? Or should it be in a private collection? Intuitively, it seems better for the painting to be in a large museum or at the least in a small one, but not in a private collection.

What brings honor to the Torah? People studying it. That given, this *sugyah* makes sense. The more people there are to hear Torah read, the more holiness will be engendered in a community. And whether that community is large or small is relatively unimportant. Numbers above ten aren't very relevant in Judaism. However, there is a great difference between ten and one, just as there is a difference between studying alone as opposed to studying with a group.

When we study alone, the text echoes only in ourselves, our own personal knowledge, memories, and understanding. When we study with others, the text strikes a different note in each person, and then each of those notes interact with one another to create something new and usually beautiful. It can be likened to a large dinner party at which each person has drunk some wine from crystal glasses. Each person's glass has a different amount of wine left. One person runs her finger along the top of the glass and it creates one note. Another person does the same, and soon there is a ringing of many different tones at the table. The tones all come from glasses of the same shape, but each one can sound different, and together or in sequence they are more beautiful than any single sound. Just so can each of us study the same text and draw quite different insights from it. In the process, we find more, and different, aspects of God's voice than we could have found alone. When we study with others, we begin to honor them for the Torah they have internalized *and* for the honor due them simply as creatures made in God's image. In our next *sugyah,* we are presented with a role model who knows how to show honor not only to God, but to people, and is rewarded for doing so.

> **GEMARA (28a):** Rabbi Zera was asked by his disciples: By virtue of what have your days been lengthened? He said to them, "Never in my life have I been harsh with my household, nor have I stepped in front of one greater than myself, nor have I meditated on the Torah in filthy alleys, nor have I gone four cubits without [repeating words of] Torah and [wearing] *tefillin,* nor have I slept in the *Beit HaMidrash* either an intentional or accidental sleep, nor have I rejoiced in the downfall of my fellow, nor have I called my fellow by his nickname, (or, as some report, 'family nickname')."

This *sugyah* is the last in a long series of answers by different rabbis to the question, "Why have you merited a long life?" As we've seen before, often the last halachic opinion or variation on a theme cited in the Talmud is meant to be the definitive one. Rabbi Zera's answer fits the theme of this chapter: showing and deserving honor in the community.

Rabbi Zera truly fulfilled the dictum from *Pirkei Avot* (4:1), "Who is honored? The one who honors others." He shows honor to his family and deference to his superiors (in Torah knowledge, obviously). He shows the same sort of honor to God and Torah that he shows to people. He does not meditate on Torah in a place of excrement, but he does do so continually in places that befit the honor of Torah thoughts. Finally, he shows honor to his colleagues, perhaps the most difficult group to show honor to, for he mentions three ways in which he honors them, instead of the two ways in which he showed honor to people, God, and Torah. He does not sleep in the *Beit HaMidrash* (that is, he listened to what his colleagues had to say). He does not rejoice when they stumble (he had his sense of competition under control), and he showed respect for the Torah that was in them by calling them by the names they wanted.

It can be easy to respect those who are not like us in some way: we are separated from them by age or position. It is easy to respect Torah and God, as well: we are connected to them, but they have aspects of holiness so rarified that they inspire awe. It is the people with whom we work most closely, and from whom we may have the greatest difficulty distinguishing ourselves, that we may most often be tempted to denigrate. It was not a Jewish philosopher who stated, "familiarity breeds contempt," but the rabbis were clearly acquainted with the phenomenon. Rabbi Zera's prescription for long life is not merely piousness. If one behaved this way—honoring others, listening to them, and respecting their opinions—one would in fact be more likely to be relaxed, have fewer enemies, and therefore live a long life.

Now we move on to the sanctity of the synagogue building. As they did when considering "accessories of holiness," the rabbis examine the extreme case of a synagogue that has fallen to ruins, in order to shed light on the proper honor due any synagogue.

**MISHNAH (28a):** Rabbi Judah said further: If a synagogue has fallen into ruins, we do not deliver funeral orations in it nor wind ropes, nor spread nets nor lay out produce on the roof [to dry] nor use it as a short cut, as its says, "And I will bring your sanctuaries unto desolation" (Leviticus 26:31) [which implies that] their holiness remains [even] when they are desolate. If grass comes up in them, it should not be plucked, so as to excite compassion.

Judaism places a premium on accepting death as a way of coping with grief. Jewish mourning rituals help us face the reality of our loss. And that same attitude holds true when a synagogue has, in effect, died. We do not pretend that it has not come to ruin by doing things in it of a prayerful nature. However, neither do we forget that once it was used for a holy purpose and that some holiness still adheres to it. Therefore, we do not use it for secular purposes, either. We let the natural processes take their course, and we let it go until we are no longer tempted to rebuild it.

How do we dissipate the collective holy energy that adheres to a place such as a synagogue or the Temple itself? What Rabbi Judah seems to be saying is, the holiness cannot ever be completely dissipated; some of that energy will always be there. Therefore, it would be disrespectful to perform secular tasks there, almost ignoring the affection and intensity that had been poured out in that place.

This may sound quite mystical, but we see examples of this phenomenon today. For example, why were there such protests when a gym was to be built on the site of the Kent State deaths or when a nunnery was to be built at Auschwitz? Or, for example, imagine that the White House and the Capitol were destroyed, but still partially standing. We wouldn't feel right about people selling fruit in the place where once laws were made and presidents stood. That is the principle at work here.

Having established the absolute baseline honor due a synagogue, even when it is in ruins, the rabbis go on to determine what honor should be shown a synagogue that is in active use.

**GEMARA (28a):** Our rabbis taught: We do not behave "lightheadedly" in synagogues. We do not eat in them, and we do not drink in them (28b), and we do not dress up in them, and we do not stroll about in them, and we do not go into them in summer to escape the heat [and we do not go into them] in the rainy season to escape the rain, and we do not deliver a private funeral address in them.

But we read [the Scriptures] in them and we repeat the *Mishnah* and we deliver public funeral addresses [in them].

While the *mishnah* gave us the baseline amount of honor due a synagogue in the form of prohibitions against using them in certain ways once they are destroyed, the Gemara gives us the flip side of the coin: how we honor synagogues that are in use. The most all-encompassing rule is that we do not behave lightheadedly in them. A synagogue is a place of intention and concentration. It is where we meet with God. Of course, this is not to imply that God is specifically located in a synagogue, but rather, it helps *us* to make contact with God when we are in a place set aside for that purpose. After listing all the things we should *not* do in a synagogue, the rabbis tell us what is appropriate to do in them: learning the Written Torah (Scriptures) and Oral Torah *(Mishnah)* and honoring those who accomplish these two tasks.

We may deliver public funeral addresses in a synagogue, but not private ones. Rashi explains that a public funeral is one held for a Torah sage. He assumes that many people would gather to eulogize such a person, and a synagogue would be suitable for this purpose, since it would be large enough to hold the crowd. The key difference between public and private funerals is that public honor is due a person who has internalized and taught Torah. Note again that the system of honor for people, places, and things in Judaism does not depend on money, power, or beauty but on the degree to which an entity holds the essence of Torah. A sage's funeral merits being held in a synagogue because the eulogy will, in describing the person's life and work, bring forth his or her connection with Torah. Thus the lessons this person learned will be taught one last time in a fitting place. This is also what will draw people to the funeral: the person's ability to make connections between the text, him or herself, and others.

The *Gemara* proceeds to give examples of public funerals and expands upon the ideas above.

**GEMARA (28b):** Reish Lakish delivered a funeral address for a certain rabbinical student who frequented the Land of Israel and who used to repeat *halachot* before twenty-four rows [of disciples]. He said, "Alas! The Land of Israel has lost a great man."

[On the other hand] there was a certain man who used to repeat *halachot, Sifra* [*midrash* on Leviticus] and *Sifrei* [*midrash* on most of Numbers and Deuteronomy] and *Tosefta,* and when he died they came and said to Rav Nachman, "Sir, will you deliver a funeral oration for him?" and he said, "How are we to deliver over him an address: 'Alas! A bag full of books has been lost!' "

Observe now the difference between the rigorous scholars of the Land of Israel and the righteous ones of Babylon *(Chasidei d'Bavel).*

To understand this *sugyah* properly, we must understand the titles and roles of the persons mentioned in it. The rabbis had a system of classifying different persons that is revealed in this *sugyah.* If we begin with the negative category, those who range from evil to merely middling, at the bottom of this group we have the *Rasha,* the evil person. A subcategory of this group is the *Naval,* a person who does not violate Jewish law, but has a clear disrespect for it. For example, the *halachah* permits us to drink wine on Shabbat, but a *Naval* would use this permission as a license to become drunk. Just above a *Rasha* is a *Bor,* a person who does not fear sin but rather only fears the punishment he will receive if he violates the *halachah.* A *Bor* may do the right thing, but for the wrong reason; not because the *Bor* has internalized the system of *mitzvot,* but because the *Bor* fears punishment. If there were no punishment, the *Bor* might well not follow the *halachah.* Above the *Bor* is the *Am Ha'arets,* literally, a "people of the land." This term refers to someone who keeps the *mitzvot* but does not know how to read and does not study. The *Am Ha'arets* is actually a good person, just unlearned.

In the positive category, the bottom rung is held by the *Ba'al Mikra,* literally, "Master of the Text," a person who knows the entire *Tanach* by heart. This person need not understand everything she knows, but merely have all of it memorized. This person's title is *Kara,* a reader. Above this is the *Ba'al Mishnah,* literally, "Master of *Mishnah,*" a person who knows the *mishnayot* of a certain school, or several schools, by heart. This person may recite the *mishnah* but may not interpret it. He is called a *Tanna,* one who repeats the *mishnah.* After the *Ba'al Mishnah* comes the *Ba'al Talmud,* literally, "Master of Talmud."

This person is allowed to interpret the *mishnayot* recited by the *Tannaim*. Such a person is called an *Amora*. After one has reached the level of *Amora*, one may aspire to become a *Ba'al Halachah*, a "master of the Law," called a *Poseik* or *Shofeit*, a law-decider or simply a judge. Such persons not only understand the Talmud, but know what to do as a result of their knowledge. Above the *Ba'al Halachah* is the *Ba'al Agadah*, the "Master of Telling." These persons not only know what to do and what the law is, but can go beyond strict adherence to the law in pursuit of a higher level of righteousness. They live their lives as examples of goodness. This going beyond the law for the sake of righteousness is called *lifnim mishurat hadin* in Hebrew. For example, if a beggar came to the door of a *Ba'al Halachah*, he might give him food and money, as is required by the law. The *Ba'al Agadah* would go beyond the law, inviting him in, bringing him to the family table for a meal, listening to him, finding ways to help him. The *Ba'al Agadah* would do this as a conscious attempt to go beyond the law, because it was right. The *Chasid* reaches a level of righteousness beyond that of even the *Ba'al Agadah*. The *Chasid*, literally "Righteous One," does what is above and beyond the letter of the law without thinking about it and without effort. For a *Chasid*, the highest level of consideration and generosity comes without effort; it is the natural thing for him or her to do. A *Chasid* sees no difference between the law *(din)* and righteousness not mandated by law *(lifnim mishurat hadin)*. They are all obligatory for her. So the *Chasid* would bring the beggar into her home and help her without thinking about it as an act of piety—simply doing it naturally. In addition, a *Chasid* *always* tells the truth. One more detail we must know before we begin to examine this *sugyah:* in the Talmud, the words *mishnah* and *halachah* may be used interchangeably.

The two men in our *sugyah* who died and are being eulogized are *Tannaim*, the "living books" who repeated material for discussion in the academies. It also seems that the man Reish Lakish eulogized, while knowledgeable, did not know quite as much as the man Rav Nachman spoke of. The first *Tanna* knew only the laws of a certain school. The second *Tanna* knew not only *Mishnah*, but the *midrashim* on Leviticus and

Deuteronomy as well as *Tosefta*. Reish Lakish did what we would normally think was the kind thing to do: he lavishly praised the man who could repeat *mishnayot* but could not understand them. Rav Nachman, on the other hand, had reached the level of *Chasid*, and as such told only the truth. The man he eulogized may have known much material, but he did not understand it. As we saw, there are many levels of knowledge and spiritual growth above the level of *Tanna* in the rabbis' system. Therefore, Rav Nachman did not want to exaggerate the man's accomplishments: he had been a good repeater of the tradition, but not a great thinker, that is, "a bag of books."

On the one hand, Rav Nachman's actions may seem cruel. Why minimize a person's accomplishments at the moment of death? However, when seen against the background of his piety, we may understand that a person who had reached Rav Nachman's level of righteousness must have seen what was good and valuable and worthy of honor in each person. There was no need to embellish the truth. The same principles operate in our own lives. Whose praise do you value more, the lavish praise of someone who you know will flatter you to build you up, or the less-extravagant praise of a perceptive person who you know always tells the truth kindly and exactly as he or she sees it?

These two cases seem to illustrate the flip side of the coin we saw when studying the *meit mitzvah*. There a person is shown the basic honor due every human being. Here the rabbis seem to be asserting that, even in death as in life, there may be a hierarchy of Torah learning and different levels of honor due it.

We may feel uncomfortable with this attitude of valuing one person's accomplishments over another's in the moment of death. And, indeed, the final line of this *sugyah* might be interpreted as an ironic statement about Rav Nachman. However, we might say that people craft their own eulogies and funerals their whole life long. Those who do not make connections with individuals or communities have lonely funerals. Those who have learned and taught, given of time and money to their families and communities, engender funerals at which there is an outpouring of love and loss. It is up to each of us to decide what kind of funeral we want to have and work backward from there. Do we want one at which people genuinely mourn because they were enriched by our lives and want more? Or do we want one where people are temporarily saddened but basically indifferent? We have the power to choose between the two.

The rabbis now extend the sphere of honor beyond the synagogue and begin to move their examination of honor into the sphere of the secular world. In the process, they affirm that our relationship with God is not dependent on any place, for God is with us wherever we are.

> **GEMARA (29a):** It has been taught: Rabbi Simon ben Yohai says: Come and see how beloved are Israel before God. For in every place to which they were exiled the *Shechinah* [God's presence] went with them.
>
> They were exiled to Egypt and the *Shechinah* was with them, as it says, "Did I surely reveal myself unto the house of your father when they were in Egypt." (1 Samuel 2:27).
>
> They were exiled to Babylon, and the *Shechinah* was with them, as it says, "For your sake I was sent to Babylon" (Isaiah 43:14).
>
> And so, when they will be redeemed in the future, the *Shechinah* will be with them, as it says, "Then the Lord your God will return [with] your captivity" (Deuteronomy 30:3). It does not say here *veheshiv* [and He shall bring back] but *veshav* [and he shall return]. This teaches us that the Holy One, blessed be He, will return with them from the places of exile.

This *sugyah* may be interpreted in the literal sense that God has been with us in our exiles and wanderings. The passage from Deuteronomy hinges on a Hebrew grammatical form of the word *return*. Here it is phrased in such a way as to imply that God is in exile with us and will come back to the Land of Israel with us. While it may be easier to make contact with God in the Land of Israel, we can do so anywhere. This *sugyah* can be interpreted in an allegorical way, as well. At many points in our lives, we may go through incredibly painful experiences and feel that God has abandoned us. However, God is with us even at these moments.

When the Divine Presence is revealed, it is so powerful a force that it creates great disturbances. Our next *sugyah* recounts what happened when God's presence was revealed to two different kinds of persons: the fathers of two great sages and a blind rabbi.

> **GEMARA (29a):** The fathers of Samuel and Levi were sitting in the synagogue which "moved and settled" in Nehardea. The *Shechinah* (God's presence) came and they heard a sound of tumult and rose and went out.
>
> Rav Sheshet [who was blind] was once sitting in the synagogue which "moved and settled" in Nehardea, when the *Shechinah* came. He did not go out, and the ministering angels came and threatened him. He turned to Him and said: Master of the Universe, if one is afflicted and one is not afflicted, who gives way to whom? God thereupon said to them [the angels]: "Leave him."

Who deserves more honor, God's presence, the fathers of Torah sages, or a blind Torah scholar? We might diagram the priority system shown here as follows:

Blind Scholar > God's presence > Fathers of Torah sages.

Ordinary people, even the fathers of great sages, leave when God's spirit approaches. Of course, this may be because directly gazing on God's presence is believed to be lethal. (This is why, for instance, we avert our faces from the priests as they recite the benediction over us, for the *Shechinah* is thought to rest upon them at that moment.) We might also note that this area of the world is wracked by earthquakes. People may have interpreted these earthquakes as the approach of God's presence. And certainly, one would not hesitate to vacate the poorly constructed buildings of those days the minute one felt an earthquake coming on. This synagogue, which "moved and settled," was reportedly made from stones brought from the site of the Temple to Babylonia.

There are many possible explanations as to why the blind Rav Sheshet's honor superseded that of the *Shechinah*. First, being blind, he might not have been susceptible to the danger engendered by gazing directly on God's presence. Another explanation could be that, being blind, he had suffered and grown out of that suffering and was strong enough, and meritorious enough, to meet the *Shechinah* directly. The implication of Rav Sheshet's remark is that affliction produces a meritorious state that the *Shechinah*, being perfect, cannot attain. Yet another explanation would harken back to the theme of this tractate: Torah and the honor due it. Being blind, Rav Sheshet had to rely on his powerful memory to remember the Torah he had learned. In other words, he had internalized a large mass of Torah, and thus honor was due him.

It is interesting that blindness figures so prominently in this tractate. It could be because the conventional forms through which we show honor: bowing, standing at attention, bestowing beautiful clothes, and so forth, may not be as relevant to blind persons. They must be shown honor in less tangible ways, through feeling and consideration. In addition, blind persons, compensating for lost sight, may be more sensitive to other kinds of input, including the spiritual. Thus they may be more in touch with God and therefore deserve more honor.

We come to our final *sugyah*, which brings together all the spheres of honor and revelation that have been discussed throughout the tractate. The intersection of text, person, and community, brought together in their proper time, are the basic ingredients of holiness. To drive the point home strongly, the segment we saw on page 4a in Chapter 1, when Moses discusses each text in its time, is repeated here and closes the chapter. This *sugyah* recaps the themes presented in each chapter.

**GEMARA (32a):** Rabbi Shefatyah further said in the name of Rabbi Johanan: If one reads the Scripture without a melody or repeats the *Mishnah* without a tune, of him the Scriptures says, "Wherefore I gave them also statutes that were not good, and ordinances whereby they should not live" (Ezekiel 20:25). Abaye strongly demurred to this: Because he cannot sing, are you to apply to him the verse, "ordinances whereby they shall not live"? No; this verse is to be applied as by Rav Mesharshya, who said: If two scholars live in the same town and do not treat one another's halachic pronouncements respectfully, of them the verse says, "I gave them also statutes that were not good and ordinances whereby they should not live."

Rabbi Parnak said in the name of Rabbi Johanan: Whoever takes hold of a scroll of the Torah naked [i.e., without a covering] is buried naked. Naked, think you? Say rather, without the covering protection of *mitzvot*. Without *mitzvot*, think you? Rather, said Abaye; he is buried without the covering protection of that [particular] *mitzvah*. Rabbi Yannai the son of the old Rabbi Yannai said in the name of the great Rabbi Yannai: It is better that the covering [of the scroll] should be rolled up [with the scroll] and not that the scroll of the Torah should be rolled up [inside the covering].

"And Moses declared unto the children of Israel the appointed seasons of the Lord" (Leviticus 23:44). It is part of their observance that [the section relating to] each one of them should be read in its season.

Our rabbis taught: Moses laid down a rule for the Israelites that they should enquire and give expositions concerning the subject of the day—the laws of Passover on Passover, the laws of Shavuot on Shavuot, and the laws of Sukkot on Sukkot.

How do we show honor to Torah on the core level of intense interaction with the text? By reading it with care and love, and in a way that shows we are remembering it and internalizing it. The rabbis felt that singing the text accomplished all these goals. To this day, the text of the Torah is sung with the "trope," the tune delineated by marks in the text. (If you have never learned trope, or learned about it, you might want to look at the Hertz Pentateuch, pp. 1045–1048, where the tunes for the trope are written out in note form.) While there is no special tune for the studying of *Mishnah* and *Gemara*, it is studied in a kind of song to this day in traditional houses of study.

While the trope is considered important, Abaye points out that the ability to sing is a rather arbitrary criterion by which to judge a Torah scholar, depending as it does on inborn talent. He prefers to move the examination of honor to the communal sphere. In particular, those who have spent a great deal of time and effort internalizing Torah and teaching it must recognize that same virtue in others. Ideally, the internalization of holiness minimizes competition and conflict; that is what truly showing honor to the Torah inside another person is about. This is the most public sphere in which Torah can be shown honor, the sphere of honor out in the real world, where halachic opinions are put into practice. This comment of Abaye corresponds to the material in Chapter 4 regarding the honor shown Torah in the world at large.

How do we show honor to the Torah in our congregations? By treating it respectfully, by keeping it covered until it is read from, so that it should not lie on a table while we ignore it, and by rolling it up correctly. The harsh decree that anyone who takes hold of a "naked" Torah will be buried naked is immediately softened to mean simply "naked" regarding this particular *mitzvah*. The statement by Rabbi Yannai is unclear and has led to many different interpretations. It seems to mean that it is better, during worship services, to roll the scroll up in a covering rather than roll it in the presence of the congregation, which would disrupt the decorum of the service. These comments by Rabbi Johanan and Rabbi Yannai seem to hearken back to our discussion of *kevod hatsibbur*, respect for the congregation, in Chapter 3, and the fact that we must obey laws of propriety when rolling the Torah during worship services.

The quote from Leviticus and its attendant commandment to read a part of the Torah for each holiday corresponds to the material in Chapter 2. There we dealt with the ritual reading of the text, and this quote, too, seems to address that issue. Leviticus 23:44, which we recite before the festival *Amidah*, comes at the end of a long section of laws concerning the different holidays (Leviticus 23:1–44). Rashi interprets the fact that this statement, "And Moses spoke of God's festivals to the Children of Israel," comes at the *end* of this long section, as opposed to the beginning, to indicate that Moses spoke of each holiday at the time when that holiday was celebrated, just as we do when we read the Torah portions for these special days. In other words, this hints at the concept that the ritual reading of text is best accomplished at its appropriate time, as we saw in Chapter 2.

Finally, the last section corresponds to Chapter 1—the direct contact with the text and the exposition of it according to the midrashic method the rabbis have shown us. We will recall that this paragraph was actually contained in Chapter 1 (4a). In both places, this *sugyah* shows us how to combine text, time, and people to create holiness.

When we finish each chapter of *Gemara,* we vow to return to it. So may we return again and again to the source of honor in our lives: Torah.

# Appendix I: The Sages

The following summaries were adapted from Mielziner's *Introduction to the Talmud* (1968), Steinsaltz's *English Reference Guide to the Talmud* (1989), his Hebrew commentary on this tractate (1983), the *Encyclopaedia Judaica* (1973), and A. Hyman's *Toldot Tannaim v'Amoraim* (1910).

**Abaye** was a fourth-generation Babylonian *Amora*. He was esteemed for his dialectical abilities as well as his integrity and gentleness. A contemporary of Rava (299–352), the two held many discussions, but Rava's opinion prevailed in all but six cases.

**Rabbi Aha** was a Palestinian *Amora* living in the fourth century. He is extensively quoted in the Jerusalem Talmud, but seldom in the Babylonian. His younger colleagues called him "the Light of Israel." He was merciful and gentle by nature. On the day of his death, it is reported that stars were visible at noontime.

**Rabbi Alexandri** was a third-century Palestinian *Amora*. He was a leading aggadist of his day. It is related that he used to go about the streets of Lydda urging people to perform good deeds.

**Rav Ashi** was a sixth-generation Babylonian *Amora* who, at the age of 20, became president of the academy of Sura, which had been deserted for about 50 years. Under his presidency, which lasted 52 years, the academy regained its renown. He had great authority and was given the title *Rabbana* ("our teacher"). He helped to compile the Talmud.

**Rav Assi** was a Babylonian *Amora* of the early third century, a contemporary of Rav and Samuel. His rulings were greatly respected throughout Babylonia.

**Bar Havu** was a scribe and seller of *tefillin* and *mezzuzot*, mentioned in *Berachot* 53b, *Baba Metsia* 29b, and *Megillah* 18b.

**Beit Hillel and Beit Shammai,** "the house of Hillel" and "the house of Shammai," existed from the end of the first century B.C.E. until the beginning of the second century C.E. In general, Beit Hillel was more lenient than its rival, Beit Shammai, but this is an oversimplification. One may safely say that Beit Shammai tended to interpret the Torah in a more literal, narrow way, whereas Beit Hillel tended to adopt a broader perspective on it. The opinions of Beit Hillel are almost always adopted over those of Beit Shammai.

**Rav Dimi** was from Nehardea and succeeded Rav Zebid in presiding over the school in Pumbedita for three years (385–388).

**Rabbi Eleazar ben Azaria,** a second-generation (80–120) *Tanna,* was a rabbi of great learning and nobility. After Rabban Gamaliel II was deposed from the presidency at Yavneh, Eleazar ben Azaria was chosen to take his place.

**Rabbi Eleazar ben Pedat** was a third-century *Amora* who died in 279. He was a member of a priestly family and was born in Babylonia. There he studied under Samuel and Rav. After the latter's death, he migrated to the Land of Israel. He was extremely poor. As well as being a great expounder of the oral law, he was a prolific and profound aggadist.

**Eleazar ben Shammua** was a *Tanna* from approximately 150 C.E. He was one of the last pupils of Rabbi Akiba and was one of the rabbis ordained by Judah ben Baba. Later *midrashim* include this Eleazar among the Ten Martyrs of the Hadrianic persecutions.

**R. Eleazar b. R. Zadok's** father was a second-generation (80–120) *Tanna*. Both Eleazar and his father were distinguished teachers in Yavneh.

**Rabbi Eliezer (ben Hyrkanos)** was a second-generation (80–120) *Tanna*. He was a faithful conservator of decisions handed down from earlier generations and opposed even the slightest modification in them. He was an adherent of Beit Shammai, and thus frequently differed with his colleagues. Being persistent in his opinion and conforming to it even in practice, he was excommunicated by his own brother-in-law, Rabban Gamaliel II.

**Elijah** was an Israelite prophet active in Israel during the reigns of Ahab and Ahaziah in the ninth century B.C.E. He fought against the worship of Baal, a Caananite god, and stressed devotion to God.

**Ezra** was a priest and scribe who played a major role in rebuilding the Temple after the return from Babylonian exile. There is some debate over when he lived; the range extends from 465 to 359 B.C.E. He provided his community with a religious basis so it could rebuild itself in Jerusalem. He adapted various laws in the Torah to the exigencies of the time.

**Haggai** was a prophet of the postexilic period; his prophecies deal mainly with the construction of the Temple. Only 38 verses of his prophecies are in our hands. They date from 520 B.C.E.

**Rav Hisda,** a second-generation (257–320) Babylonian *Amora,* was a disciple of Rav. He became head of the academy in Sura when he was 80 years old and remained in that office for 10 years.

**Rabbi Hiyya bar Abba** immigrated from Babylonia and became a disciple of Rabbi Jochanan. He was a Palestinian *Amora* of the second generation (279–320). He was a distinguished teacher, inclined toward rigorous views, and quite poor.

**Rav Huna** (b. 212, d. 297) was a second-generation Babylonian *Amora.* He was president of the Academy at Sura for 40 years and had 800 disciples. He was highly revered for his great learning and his noble character. He enjoyed an undisputed authority to which even some Palestinian teachers submitted.

**Rabbi Isaac** was a *Tanna* from Babylonia in the middle of the second century. He moved to the Land of Israel, where he debated the disciples of R. Ishmael. He also engaged in mystical studies. He is not mentioned in the *Mishnah,* but is often cited in *beraitot.*

**Rabbi Jeremiah,** a native of Babylonia, was a third-generation (320–359) Palestinian *Amora* and a disciple of R. Zeira. In his younger days, he indulged in posing puzzling questions of little import, probably intending to ridicule the dialectical methods used in the academies. For this reason, he was expelled from the academy. He then moved to Palestine and was better appreciated there, being acknowledged as a great authority.

**Rabbi Jochanan bar Napacha** is usually called simply Rabbi Jochanan. Born about 199, he died in 279 and was a first-generation Palestinian *Amora.* He founded his own academy, which became the principal seat of learning in the Land of Israel.

He was regarded as the chief *Amora* of Palestine, due to his great mental powers.

**Jonathan ben Uzziel** lived in the first century B.C.E. and the first century C.E. An outstanding pupil of Hillel, he translated the Prophets into Aramaic (*Baba Batra* 134a; *Sukkah* 28a).

**Rabbi Jose (ben Chalafta),** a fourth-generation (139–165 C.E.) *Tanna,* was a disciple of Rabbi Akiba. He was an outstanding and fair-minded scholar; always trying to take every aspect of a problem into account. So great was his scholarship that whenever there is a conflict between him and his contemporaries, Rabbis Meir, Judah, and Simon, his opinion is always adopted. In addition to his intellectual gifts, he was also humble and righteous. It is said that Elijah was revealed to him every day.

**Rabbi Jose ben Hanina** was a Palestinian *Amora* of the second half of the third century. He was an important member of the academy of Tiberias and colleague and pupil of Jochanan. He tended to urge compromise rather than adherence to the strict letter of the law when judging cases. He was a great aggadist and outstanding preacher. He was apparently wealthy, and his children died during his lifetime. (There is also a *Tanna* by this name.)

**Rav Joseph ben Hiyya** (d. 333 C.E.), a Babylonian *Amora,* headed the Pumbedita academy for two and a half years. Hundreds of his sayings are found throughout the Talmud. He was called *Sinai,* meaning a scholar with wide knowledge. He also delved into mysticism. He was renowned for his high ethical standards and especially for his humility. He was wealthy and supported 400 of his pupils.

**Joshua son of Nun** was Moses' successor and led the Israelite conquest of the land of Canaan. He led the battle against Amalek after the children of Israel left Egypt (Exodus 17:9–14). He is portrayed as both a military leader and a prophet.

**Rabbi Joshua (ben Chanania)** belonged to the second generation of *Tannaim* (80–120). Joshua often had discussions with Rabbi Eliezer, his rational and conciliatory style contrasting with Rabbi Eliezer's unyielding conservatism. It was on Rabbi Joshua's account that Rabban Gamaliel II was removed from office.

**Rabbi Joshua ben Levi** was a second-generation (219–279) Palestinian *Amora* (born about 180, died 260). He is regarded as a great authority in the law, and his decisions often prevail over those of Rabbi Jochanan and Reish Lakish, his two great contemporaries. He was also a prolific aggadist. He presided over an academy in Lydda. It is said that, on one occasion, his prayer for rain was efficacious, and this later gave rise to many mystical legends about him.

**Rabbi Judah bar Ilai** was a *Tanna* of the mid-second century. Where R. Judah is mentioned without a patronymic in the *Mishnah,* it refers to him. He was a great halachic authority. He warned that giving an accurate Aramaic translation of the Bible was difficult, saying, "He who translates a verse literally is a liar, and he who adds to it is a libeler" (*Tosefta, Megillah* 3:41). He was one of Rabbi Akiba's disciples and was known for his piety, modesty, and prudence. His opinions carry great authority and are quoted throughout the *Mishnah* and *baraitot.* The *midrash Sifra* is ascribed to him.

**Rabbi Judah ben Baba,** a third-generation (120–139) *Tanna,* was also called the *Chasid* ("the righteous one") on account of his piety. He was a distinguished teacher and was martyred by the Romans for ordaining seven disciples of Rabbi Akiba as rabbis.

**Rav Judah (bar Yecheskel),** a second-generation (257–320) Babylonian *Amora,* was a disciple of both Rav's and Shmuel's. He founded the academy in Pumbedita, and also headed the academy at Sura for the two years before his death in 299.

**Rabbi Judah HaNasi,** simply called Rabbi, or Our Rabbi, a fifth-generation (165–200) *Tanna,* was a son of the patriarch R. Simon ben Gamaliel II. He was well versed not only in the traditional law, but also in secular subjects, such as the Greek language. He became the chief authority of his generation. Although personally wealthy, he lived simply and sustained many students by his charity. He is said to have had friendly relations with one of the Roman emperors. He completed the compilation of the *Mishnah* begun by Rabbi Akiba.

**Levi,** a Palestinian *Amora* of the third quarter of the third century, is usually mentioned without his patronymic, but it may be Lahma or Hama. He was primarily a talented aggadist. There are no *halachot* cited in his name. He claimed the ability to link together texts from different sections of the Bible and penetrate their inner meaning (*Song of Songs Rabbah* 1:10). He frequently explained difficult words in the biblical text by referring to Arabic words.

**Malachi,** a prophet, was a contemporary of Nehemiah, who rebuilt the Temple after the people's return from exile in the middle of the fifth century B.C.E.

**Rabbi Meir** was a fourth-generation (139–165) *Tanna*. His ordination was confirmed by Rabbi Judah ben Baba, after having been ordained by Rabbi Akiba quite early in his (Meir's) career. He was the most prominent of Akiba's disciples and continued Akiba's work in arranging the material of the Oral Law according to subjects. In this way he helped prepared the great *Mishnah* compilation of Judah HaNasi.

**Men of the Great Assembly.** See Glossary.

**Rav Nachman bar Isaac,** a third-generation (320–375) Babylonian *Amora,* was president of the academy in Pumbedita for four years (352–356) and left no remarkable traces of his activity.

**Rav Nachman (ben Jacob)** is usually referred to without his patronymic. A Babylonian *Amora* and leading personality of his time, he died around 320 C.E. He was born in Nehardea and married into the family of the exilarch (*Hullin* 124a). He regarded himself of sufficient standing as a judge to try cases on his own (*Sanhedrin* 5a).

**R. Nehemiah** was one of Rabbi Akiba's last disciples. His controversies are mostly with Rabbi Judah bar Ilai. He collected tannaitic teachings into the *Tosefta.*

**Onkelos,** like Aquila, who translated the Bible into Greek, was a proselyte who lived in the second century C.E. He translated the Bible into Aramaic. Similar or identical incidents are told of these two men in the Talmud, and some believe them to be the same person.

**Our Rabbi.** See Rabbi Judah HaNasi.

**Rav Papa (bar Chanan),** a fifth-generation (320–375) Babylonian *Amora,* was a disciple of Abaye and Rava. He adopted their dialectical method, but did not possess their ingenuity and independence in applying it.

**Rav Papi** is the name of two *Amoraim.* One is the Babylonian *Amora* of the fourth century who became the greatest *Amora* of his time. He was a wealthy landowner. The other Rav Papi is a

Palestinian *Amora* of the fourth century. Most of the sayings recorded in his name are aggadic, some in the name of his teacher, Rabbi Levi.

**Rabba bar bar Chana** was a Babylonian *Amora* of the second generation (257–320). He attended Rabbi Jochanan's academy in Palestine and then returned to Babylonia. He is noted for the many allegorical narratives ascribed to him in the Talmud.

**Rabba (bar Nachmani)** was a Babylonian *Amora* who lived from 270 to 330. He was a disciple of Rav Chisda, among others, and had great analytical and intellectual powers. He became the head of the academy of Pumbedita and attracted large crowds at his lectures there. He lived a life of poverty and suffered a tragic death, persecuted by the Babylonian authorities for allegedly encouraging tax evasion.

**Rav's** real name is Abba Areca. He was born about 175 and died in 247 and was a first-generation Babylonian *Amora*. He was regarded as a semi-*Tanna* and was thus able, in some instances, to dispute some opinions accepted in the *Mishnah,* a privilege not accorded to any other *Amora*.

**Rava,** a third-generation Babylonian *Amora,* was born in 299 and died in 352. He was a colleague of Abaye and developed dialectical powers that soon surpassed all his contemporaries. His rulings overrule Abaye's in all but six cases in the Talmud. His academy in Machuza supplanted all others in Babylonia.

**Reish Lakish.** See Simon ben Lakish.

**Mar Samuel** (or Shmuel) was born about 180 in Nehardea and died there in 257. A first-generation Babylonian *Amora* (219–257), like his colleague Rav, he went to Palestine and there became a disciple of Judah HaNasi, although Judah did not ordain him. Samuel was interested in medicine and astronomy. Although he and Rav often differed on questions of law, their relationship was friendly. After Rav's death in 247, Samuel became the highest religious authority in Babylonia.

**R. Samuel b. Judah** was, during the first half of the fourth century, one of the *nehutei,* "one who goes down," a group of rabbis who shuttled between the academies in the Land of Israel and Babylonia in order to bring the teachings of the former to the latter.

**R. Samuel b. Nahmani** was a Palestinian *Amora* of the late third and early fourth centuries C.E. He was known as an aggadist, and his halachic opinions are also recorded in both the Babylonian and Palestinian Talmuds.

**Rav Sheshet,** a Babylonian *Amora* of the second generation, opposed hair-splitting methods of study, and often opposed R. Chisda. He was blind and thus had to depend on his powerful memory.

**Shimon bar Abba** was a second-generation (279–320) Palestinian *Amora*. He was probably the brother of Chiya bar Abba. Both immigrated to Palestine from Babylonia, were distinguished teachers, were very poor, and were disciples of Rabbi Jochanan. Both were inclined to be rigorous in deciding the *halachah*.

**Rabbi Shimon b. Eleazar** was a second-century *Tanna* and contemporary of Judah haNasi. His *halachot* are often stated as general principles. He is frequently quoted in the *aggadah*.

**Rabban Shimon ben Gamaliel** was the son of Rabban Gamaliel of Yavneh and was *Nasi* during the first half of the second century C.E. He did not enjoy the same status as his father, but some hundred *halachot* are quoted in his name in the *Mishnah* and still more in the *beraitot* and *Tosefta*. He was the father of Judah HaNasi, who compiled the *Mishnah*.

**Simeon Ha-Pakuli** was a *Tanna* of the late first and early second century C.E. He was one of the scholars in Yavneh during the time of Gamaliel II. According to Rashi, his name refers to his occupation as a seller of cotton tufts, *pakuli*. He is mentioned here and in *Berachot* 28b.

**Rabbi Simeon bar Yochai** was a fourth-generation (139–165) *Tanna* from the Galilee. (According to Steinsaltz, he was a fifth-generation (135–170) *Tanna*.) He was one of Rabbi Akiba's most distinguished disciples. Persecuted by the Romans, he hid himself in a cave for several years with his son, eating only carob to sustain himself. He opened an academy in Tekoa in the Galillee once the Roman government stopped persecuting him. He followed the school of Rabbi Ishmael rather than Rabbi Akiba. He is regarded as the author of *Sifrei*, the *midrash* on Deuteronomy.

**Rabbi Simon ben Lakish** (known as **Reish Lakish**) lived in Palestine and was one of the first generation of *Amoraim* (219–279 C.E.). Before becoming a scholar, he was a gladiator for the Romans. He had extraordinary intellectual and analytical gifts. He was not only good friends with Rav Jochanan, but his brother-in-law, as well.

**Sofrim,** or scribes, were a class of scholars who lived and worked from the time of Ezra until the time of Simon the Just, i.e., until the end of the Great Assembly. They were active during the period of Persian rule and laid down many of the principles and norms in the Oral Law.

**Ulla bar Rav** was a Palestinian *Amora* of the second half of the third century. He studied under Jochanan bar Napacha, Reish Lakish, and Eleazar ben Pedat. He was extremely strict in his interpretation of religious laws and denigrated decisions he disliked. He was greatly respected in the Land of Israel and in Babylonia, which he visited frequently. He felt the tragedy of the destruction of the Temple deeply. He died in Babylon, survived by his only son, Rabba.

**The Watchmen** (The Prophets) were individuals through whom God made known the Divine will. These spokesmen for God, such as Moses, Isaiah, Jeremiah, and Ezekiel, were chosen by God and conveyed God's word to the people, sometimes against their will. The prophets, whose works are collected in the second part of the *Tanach,* prophesied from the days of Samuel (approximately 1000 B.C.E.) until Haggai, Zechariah, and Malachi (mid-fifth century B.C.E.).

**Yannai Rabah (the Great)** was an early third-century Palestinian *Amora.* Apparently he was descended from the high priest, Eli, and was quite wealthy. Yannai was a pupil of Judah Ha-Nasi. He was pious, extremely considerate of the poor, and had a realistic view of life.

**Zechariah,** a prophet in Palestine after the Jewish exiles had returned from Babylon, urged the Jewish people to rebuild the Temple.

**Rabbi Zera** was a second-generation (279–320) Palestinian *Amora.* Originally from Babylonia, he did not like the hair-splitting techniques of study used in the academies there and emigrated to Palestine, where he was ordained.

**Mar Zutra** was an *Amora* of the fourth generation (375–427) in Pumbedita, Babylonia.

# Appendix II: Halachah

The following is a translation of Steinsaltz's summary of the *halachah* for this tractate.

## Chapter 1

**2a:** Cities whose walls date from the days of Joshuah ben Nun (even if they do not have a wall today) read the *Megillah* on the fifteenth of *Adar*) and the rest of the Jewish community reads it on the fourteenth of *Adar* (*Shulchan Aruch, Orach Chayim* 688:1, 3). A *Beit Din* that made a proclamation of any strength cannot be overturned by a *Beit Din* that comes after them. See Rambam, *Sefer Shoftim, Hilchot Mamrim* 2:2.

**3b:** One must abandon Torah study to accompany the dead to the grave (*Shulchan Aruch, Yoreh Deah* 361:1).

Even though we push aside most of the *mitzvot* of the Torah in order to read the *Megillah*, the burial of a *meit mitzvah* pushes aside the reading of the *Megillah*. And there are those who say it need not even necessarily be a *meit mitzvah*. A Torah sage is due the honor given a *meit mitzvah* (*Shulchan Aruch, Orach Chayim* 687:2).

Even a High Priest or Nazirite, and even one going to circumcise his son or slaughter his Passover offering, is obligated to push aside the *mitzvah* he is doing and attend to the needs of a *meit mitzvah* (*Shulchan Aruch, Yoreh Deah* 374:1).

**5a:** One may read the *Megillah* as an individual on the correct day (the fourteenth of *Adar*, or the fifteenth for walled cities), but it is preferable to read it in a *minyan* (a group of ten) (*Shulchan Aruch, Orach Chayim* 690:18).

A place without ten permanent *batlanim* in the synagogue is judged to be a village, not a city (Ramban, *Sefer Zmanim, Hilchot Megillah* 1:8).

**7a:** The five *megillot* (Song of Songs, Ruth, Lamentations, Ecclesiastes, and Esther) have the holiness of Scriptures and make the hands impure (Rambam, *Sefer Taharah, Hilchot Avot HaTumah* 9:4).

**7b:** A person is obligated to become so intoxicated on Purim that he cannot tell the difference between "Cursed is Haman" and "Blessed is Mordecai," for the law is according to Rabba. And there are those who say that we are not required to become so intoxicated, but rather simply drink more than is our custom. And there are those who say that one should drink until one falls asleep, for then one can no longer tell the difference between "Cursed is Haman" and "Blessed is Mordecai," and so fulfills his obligation (*Shulchan Aruch* 695:2).

**8b:** *Tefillin* and *mezzuzot* are written only in the Assyrian script (Rambam, *Sefer Ahavah, Hilchot Tefillin* 1:19).

**9b:** A *Sefer Torah* may be written in Greek and it has holiness. However, since the Greek language has changed, we no longer write a *Sefer Torah* in Greek (Rambam, *Sefer Taharah, Hilchot Avot Hatumot* 9:7).

## Chapter 2

**17a:** One who reads the *Megillah* with the verses in the wrong order, or by heart, has not fulfilled the obligation to read the *Megillah* (*Shulchan Aruch, Orach Chayim* 690:6).

**18a:** If a *Megillah* was written in Aramaic or another language, one has not fulfilled one's obligation unless one is familiar with that language (*Shulchan Aruch, Orach Chayim* 690:9).

One may write the *Megillah* in any style of handwriting, but some say it must be in Assyrian script, and that is our custom now (*Shulchan Aruch, Orach Chayyim* 690:9).

**18b:** It is forbidden to write even one letter of Scripture by heart (*Shulchan Aruch, Yoreh Deah* 294:2).

The law follows Rabbi Jeremiah: *tefillin* do not need lines (*shirtut*), while *mezzuzot* must have them (*Shulchan Aruch, Yoreh Deah* 288:8). However, today the custom is that *tefillin* also are written with lines (*Shulchan Aruch, Orach Chayim* 32:6).

**19b:** Everyone who is obligated to read the *Megillah* (i.e., men and women) can fulfill the obligation of its reading for others. Some authorities say women cannot fulfill the obligation on behalf of men. Most authorities rule that a deaf person cannot fulfill this obligation for others, but once such a person has done so, it counts (*Shulchan Aruch, Orach Chayim* 689:2).

**19b:** When composing the parchments of a *Sefer Torah* and/or *Megillah,* one must leave a measure of space free at the beginning and end so that it should not be torn (*Shulchan Aruch, Orach Chayim* 691:7 and *Yoreh Deah* 278:1).

## Chapter 3

**21a:** One may read the *Megillah* either sitting or standing, but the blessing over it must be said while standing. However, we do not read the *Megillah* sitting because of the honor of the congregation. However, if a congregation wants to take pity on a reader, it may do so (*Shulchan Aruch, Orach Chayim* 690:1).

On Mondays and Thursdays, three persons, not more, read in the Torah, and there is no *Haftarah* from a Prophet (*Shulchan Aruch, Orach Chayim* 135:1).

On Rosh Chodesh, four read in the Torah, and we neither add nor subtract from this number, and there is no *Haftarah* from a prophet (*Shulchan Aruch, Orach Chayim* 423:1). On a Festival, two *Sefer Torahs* are read. In the first, five people read and the second is the *Maftir*. It is permissible to add to the number of readers on a Festival, especially on Simchat Torah, when many *aliyot* are added until everyone has had a chance to read (*Shulchan Aruch, Orach Chayim* 282:1).

On most *Shabbatot*, one *Sefer Torah* is read. On special *Shabbatot*, two are read from. Seven read from one Torah scroll, and the *maftir* reads from the second. The custom now is that no additional readers are added to this number (*Shulchan Aruch, Orach Chayim* 282:1).

**21b:** We say three blessings before the reading of the

*Megillah:* ". . . for the reading of the *Megillah*"; ". . . who did miracles for our Ancestors in those days at this time"; and ". . . who has kept us alive, sustained us, and brought us to this time." Today, Ashkenazim repeat the *shehechiyanu* in the morning, as do some Sephardim. And the custom is to recite the blessing after the *Megillah* and it ends, ". . . who avenges Israel on all their enemies, the God who saves" (*Shulchan Aruch, Orach Chayim* 692:1).

**23a:** Everyone can be called to the Torah as one of the seven *aliyot* on Shabbat, even a woman. However, the sages ruled that women may not do so, nor may a minor, except for *maftir* or on Simchat Torah (*Shulchan Aruch, Orach Chayim* 282:3).

**23b:** We do not have one person stand and say *kaddish*, *barechu* and the *kedushah*, except in the presence of ten persons (*Shulchan Aruch, Orach Chayim* 69:1).

We do not stand to say the *Amidah* in public before the ark except in the presence of ten persons (*Shulchan Aruch, Orach Chayim* 69:1).

The *Cohanim* do not lift up their hands for the priestly benediction except in a *minyan* (and they may count as part of that *minyan*) (*Shulchan Aruch, Orach Chayim* 128:1). The Torah is not read without a *minyan*. However, if the reading was started with a *minyan* and a few people left, the reading may be completed (*Shulchan Aruch, Orach Chayim* 143:1).

Likewise, a *Haftarah* cannot be read without a *minyan* (Rambam, *Sefer Ahavah, Hilchot Tefillah* 8:4).

**25b:** Not every text of Scripture is translated in public. The story of Reuben (35:22), the Priestly blessing (Numbers 6:24-26) and the story of the calf from "And Moses said to Aaron" to "And Moses saw the people, etc." (Exodus 32:21-25) and also the verse "And God plagued the people" (Exodus 32:35) are not translated. And similarly, in the story of Amnon (2 Samuel 13), the place where it says of him "Ammon the son of David" (2 Samuel 13:1) is read but not translated. (Rambam, *Mishneh Torah, Sefer Ahavah, Hilchot Tefillah* 12:12). Even though *mocking* is generally prohibited, it is permissible to *mock* at idolatry (*Shulchan Aruch, Yoreh Deah* 147:5).

## Chapter 4

**26a:** If one sold the wrappings for scrolls, one may buy books with the money (i.e., a *Chumash*, Prophets, or Writings). If one sold such books, one may buy a *Sefer Torah* with the money. However, we do not lower in holiness, even with the money left over from the original sale (*Shulchan Aruch, Orach Chayim* 153:2).

**26b:** The implements of a *mitzvah* that cannot be reused for that *mitzvah*, such as worn out *tsitsit*, need not be stored away, but may be thrown away. However, it is meritorious to store them away or use them for some other *mitzvah* (*Shulchan Aruch, Orach Chayim* 21:1).

Implements of holiness, such as an ark or a Torah case, are stored away (*Shulchan Aruch, Orach Chayim* 154:3).

**27a:** One is allowed to make a House of Study out of a synagogue, and is allowed to sell a synagogue in order to build a House of Study. However, one may not turn a House of Study into a synagogue. However, today, when synagogues and Houses of Study are joined, they are considered Houses of Study (*Shulchan Aruch, Orach Chayim* 153:1).

It is prohibited to sell a *Sefer Torah*, although it is permissible to sell individual holy books, even if one has many *Sifrei Torah*, and even if one has nothing to eat (unless in extremely dire circumstances). It is even forbidden to sell an old *Sefer Torah* in order to by a new one. However, in order to study Torah, or marry a wife (if he had nothing else with which to become betrothed), or redeem a captive, or provide healing for a sick person who is in danger of dying, one may sell a *Sefer Torah*. However, it is considered a great *mitzvah* to contribute to such needy causes so that the *Sefer Torah* need not be sold (*Shulchan Aruch, Yoreh Deah* 270:1).

**28a:** It is prohibited to repeat words of Torah in a place of excrement (*Shulchan Aruch, Orach Chayim* 85:2).

It is prohibited to sleep in the *Beit HaMidrash* purposefully, but if one accidentally fell asleep it is tolerated. However, it is considered a quality of piety not to sleep in the *Beit HaMidrash* at all (*Shulchan Aruch, Yoreh Deah* 246:16).

# Glossary

**Acrostic:** Alphabetically ordered poem or song, or one in which the first letter of each verse or line spells out a word. For example, the first letter of each verse of the *Shabbat* hymn, *Lecha Dodi*, spells out the name of its composer, Shlomo HaLevi.

**Adar:** A Jewish month in late winter, early spring. When a leap year occurs, there are two months of *Adar*. The reading of the special *haftarah* portions (see The Four Portions) and Purim are observed in the second Adar in such a year.

**Aggadah/Aggadot:** Stories in the Talmud text as opposed to material pertaining directly to Jewish law. Differs from *midrash* (see below) in that these stories are not necessarily related to a scriptural text.

**Aggadic:** Of, or concerning, *aggadah*.

**Aggadist:** A teller of stories. One who interprets the Torah text rather than concentrating on *halachah*, "Jewish law."

**Aliyah/Aliyot:** Literally, "going up." The act of saying the blessings over the Torah reading during worship services or actually reading from the Torah. This word may also refer to the person who has a synagogue honor. In addition, other honors during the service (e.g., opening the ark) are called *aliyot*.

**Amidah/Amidot/Tefillah/Tefillot/Shemoneh Esrei:** Literally, "standing," "the prayer," and "eighteen." The prayer par excellence in Judaism. On weekdays, it contains nineteen benedictions. It is said standing three times each day.

**Amora/Amoraim:** The sages who expounded the *mishnah*, thereby composing the *Gemara*. The *Gemara* and *Mishnah*

141

together form the Talmud. The period of the *Amoraim* extends from the death of Judah HaNasi until the Babylonian Talmud was compiled, i.e., from the end of the third to the end of the fifth century. *Amoraim* lived in both Palestine and Babylonia.

**Anshei K'neset HaGedolah:** Literally, "the men of the Great Assembly." This Great Assembly was a legislative body of 120 men that functioned during and after the Persian period of Jewish history, approximately 500–200 B.C.E. This body developed many of the norms and practices of Judaism.

**Apocrypha:** A Greek word meaning "Hidden Things." A collection of ancient books that were not included in the *Tanach* but were collected by other religious traditions. The Apocrypha contains the First and Second Books of Esdras, Tobit, Judith, The Rest of the Chapters of the Book of Esther, the Wisdom of Solomon, Ecclesiasticus (Ben Sira), Baruch, A Letter of Jeremiah, The Song of the Three, Daniel and Susanna, Daniel, Bel and the Snake, The Prayer of Manasseh, and the First and Second Books of the Maccabees.

**Aramaic:** One of the languages used in the Talmud. It is similar in some ways to Hebrew. It developed after Hebrew and was the language of the general population in the days of the *Amoraim.*

**Asya:** This may be a district outside Palestine in Asia Minor, although some maintain that it is on the east of the Jordan River near the Dead Sea.

**B.C.E.:** Before the Common Era, i.e., B.C.

**Ba'al Korei/Ba'alei Korei:** Literally, "the master of the reading," i.e., the person who reads from the Torah in synagogue.

**Baraita/Baraitot:** Literally, "external." A source from the *Tannaitic* era that was not included in the *Mishnah* of Rabbi Judah HaNasi.

**Bat Kol:** Literally, "A Voice from Heaven." There are four possible meanings for this concept: 1. Popular opinion. 2. Listening to children, especially asking them what verse they are reading and taking it as prophecy. 3. An echo: *bat kol* can be taken literally as "the daughter of a sound."

4. *Bat Kol Min HaShamayim:* A voice from heaven. This is true revelation; however, it cannot be used as a basis for adjudicating Jewish law.

**Beit Din:** Literally, "A House of Judgment." A general term for a judicial body in the area of *halachah* that usually has at least three judges. The *Beit Din* regulates the affairs of the community as well as adjudicating civil and criminal matters.

**Beit HaKneset:** Literally, "The House of Meeting." A synagogue.

**Beit HaMidrash:** Literally, "The House of Expounding." An academy of rabbinic learning.

**Beit Hillel:** Literally, "The House of Hillel." The school that developed to expound the ideas of Hillel, one of the last of the *zugot*. The laws of this school are almost always adopted over those of *Beit Shammai*. These two houses existed during the first generation of *Tannaim*, i.e., 10–80 C.E.

**Beit Shammai:** Literally, "The House of Shammai." The school that developed to expound the ideas of Shammai, one of the last of the *zugot*.

**Bimah:** Literally, "a stage, or platform." The raised dais from which Torah is read in the synagogue.

**C.E.:** The Common Era, i.e., A.D.

**Chag/Chagim:** Literally, "Festival." The festivals ordained in the Torah—Passover, Sukkot, and Shavuot, as well as Rosh HaShanah and Yom Kippur—share many of the same restrictions that apply to Shabbat, such as the prohibitions against carrying items from one domain to another, and so forth.

**Chatimah/Chatimot:** Literally, "a seal." This is the phrase that begins *Baruch atah Adonai . . . ,* "Blessed are You, *Adonai* . . ." that summarizes, and closes, a blessing.

**Chol HaMoed:** The intermediate days of a festival, i.e., between the first and last days of Pesach and Sukkot. They are not full holidays, but they are not ordinary weekdays, either. Work may be done on these days.

**Chumash:** A book containing the first five books of the Bible— Genesis, Exodus, Leviticus, Numbers, and Deuteronomy.

**Cubit:** (Hebrew: *Amah/Amot*): A measure of length. Estimates of its length vary from 18–24 inches.

**Denar/Denarii:** A type of coin mentioned in the Talmud.

**Drash:** The act of making an exposition of a biblical text.

**Drashah/Drashot:** An exposition of a biblical text.

**Ecclesiastes:** One of the five scrolls. A book of Wisdom literature.

**The Four Portions:** These are four passages from the Torah read on four Sabbaths each year (one per Sabbath), two before Purim and two before Pesach: (1) *Parshat Shekalim* (Exodus 30:11–16), "The Portion of the Shekels," read on the Sabbath preceding the month of *Adar,* or on the first day of that month, regarding the obligation for everyone to contribute a half shekel to the central sacrificial cult; (2) *Parshat Zachor* (Deuteronomy 25:17–19), "The Portion of Remembrance," in which we are commanded to re-member Amalek, read on the Sabbath before Purim; (3) *Parshat Parah* (Numbers 19:1–22), "The Portion of the Cow," the purification ritual of the red heifer, read on the Sabbath after Purim; and (4) *Parshat HaChodesh* (Exodus 12:1–20), "The Portion of the Month," details the laws of the Passover sacrifice, read before Pesach.

**Gelilah:** Literally, "rolling." The task of rolling up the scroll of the Torah and dressing it once it has been read in synagogue.

**Gemara:** The commentary on the *Mishnah* composed by the *Amoraim.* It contains *Baraitot, aggadot,* and *Amoraic* discus-sions. The Babylonian Gemara was formulated between 200 and 500 C.E. The Yerushalmi, the Talmud of the Land of Israel, was formulated around 400 C.E.

**Gematria:** Numerology. The system of biblical interpretation using the numerical value of each Hebrew letter to un-cover hidden meanings.

**Genizah/Genizot:** Literally, "Hiding place or Archive." A place where holy books, documents that contain God's name, or other holy items may be properly stored away.

**Gezeira Shava:** "An equivalent pronouncement." An analogy of expressions based on identical or similar words occur-ring in two different passages of Scripture.

**Gnosticism:** A dualistic religion that holds that there are two gods, a god of good and a god of evil.

**Great Assembly:** The *K'neset HaGedolah*. See *Anshei K'neset HaGedolah*.

**Haftarah:** From the root "dismiss, release." A reading from the Prophets that follows the Torah readings on *Shabbatot* and Festivals.

**Hagbah:** Literally, "lifting." The act of lifting high the scroll of the Torah once it has been read in synagogue and showing it to the congregation.

**Hagiographa:** The Writings. The third part of the *Tanach* containing the Psalms, Proverbs, Job, the Five Scrolls, Daniel, Ezra, Nehemiah, and Chronicles.

**Halachah:** "The Way." Jewish law.

**Halachah l'Moshe miSinai:** Literally, "A law of Moses from Sinai." An authoritative law handed down from earlier generations.

**Hallel:** Literally "praise." The *Hallel* consists of Psalms 113–118 and is recited on the first night(s) and day(s) of Pesach, Shavuot, Sukkot, Shemini Atzeret, Simchat Torah, and Hanukkah. An abridged form of the Hallel is recited on *Rosh Chodesh* and the intermediate and final days of Pesach.

**Hermeneutics:** Methodological principles of interpretation of the biblical text. These include such rules as the *gezeira shava, kal vachomer,* etc. The thirteen hermeneutic rules of Rabbi Ishmael are included in the morning service that is recited each day.

**Hesped:** A eulogy for the dead.

**Kalut Rosh:** Literally, "Light-headedness" Frivolousness, insufficient seriousness. The opposite of *Koved Rosh,* "heavy-headedness" or seriousness.

**Kal vaChomer:** An *a fortiori* inference. A logical comparison between two cases, one lenient *(kal)* and the other strict *(chomer):* "If A, then certainly B." For example, "If you have run with foot-soldiers and they have wearied you, how can you contend with horses?" (Jeremiah 12:5). (See Steinsaltz's Reference Volume, p. 153, for a good, lengthy discussion of this concept.)

**Kareit:** From the root "cutting." Often interpreted as premature death brought on by God as a punishment for sin.

**Kefar Gibboraya:** Some say this is Kfar Nvorya, Navor Chayil, a town north of Tsefat that has many ancient congregations.

**Lifnim Mishurat haDin:** Literally, "Inside the line of justice." Going beyond the requirements of law for the sake of fairness or righteousness.

**Maftir:** Related to the word *Haftarah*. The short section at the end of a weekly or festival Torah portion that is reread once it has been included in the regular *aliyot*. The person who says the blessing over this short portion then proceeds to read the *Haftarah*.

**Media:** Media is the country of the Medes who lived in the mountainous area of Iran and the northeastern and eastern region of Mesopotamia. Media was eventually incorporated into the Persian Empire.

**Megillah/Megillot:** Literally, "a Scroll." It usually refers to the five *megillot* in the *Tanach:* Song of Songs, Eicha (Lamentations), Kohelet (Ecclesiastes), Esther, and Ruth.

**Meit Mitzvah:** A corpse that has no one to bury it. The burial of a *meit mitzvah* is an important religious duty.

**Men of the Great Assembly:** See *Anshei K'neset HaGedolah.*

**Mezuzah/Mezuzot:** "Doorpost." A parchment on which are written the words of Deuteronomy 6:4–9 and Deuteronomy 11:13–21. The parchment is then affixed to the doorposts of a dwelling.

**Midrash/Midrashim:** Expositions of biblical texts.

**Minchah:** "Afternoon." The afternoon recitation of the *Amidah.*

**Min/Minim:** "Kind, Species." A heretic, especially members of early Jewish Christian sects or Gnostics.

**Minor:** (Hebrew: *Katan*) A person who has not reached maturity, now generally accepted as up to the age of 12 for girls and 13 for boys.

**Mishloach Manot:** Literally, "the Sending of Portions." One of the principle *mitzvot* of Purim. The practice of exchanging gifts of food in honor of the holiday.

**Mishnah/Mishnayot:** "Teaching." Refers to the collection of tannaitic learning compiled by Rabbi Judah HaNasi in 200

C.E. and also to individual segments within that compilation.

**Mitzvah:** "Commandment." A deed that one must perform or an action one must refrain from doing that is derived from the Torah or from a dictate of the rabbis.

**Musaf:** "Addition." The additional public sacrifices brought on Shabbat, the New Moon, and Festivals when the Temple stood. Also the name of the extra service recited on days when this sacrifice would have been brought.

**Nehardea:** Nehardea was a town in Babylonia with one of the region's oldest Jewish communities. Its *yeshivah*, headed during one period by Shmuel, was one of the oldest in Babylonia. The city lay near the border between the Roman and Persian empires, and thus was frequently caught in wars between them. It was completely destroyed in 259 C.E. but was thereafter resettled by Jews.

**Olam HaBa:** "The World to Come." The pleasant realm in the afterlife where the righteous are rewarded.

**Onkelos:** See Sages.

**Parsang:** A Parsang is a Persian mile; about 2.4 miles.

**Pentateuch:** The first five books of the Bible: Genesis, Exodus, Leviticus, Numbers, and Deuteronomy.

**Pentecost:** The holiday of Shavuot, which means "weeks." This holiday celebrates the offering of the First Fruits in Jerusalem and the giving of the Ten Commandments. The Book of Ruth is read on this day.

**Persia:** The Persian Empire's base coincides with the province of Fars in modern Iran. (See *Encyclopaedia Judaica*, vol. 13, pp. 303–304, for a map of the area.)

**Pesach:** "To pass over." The Festival in the spring that celebrates the Exodus from Egypt. This holiday marks the end of winter. The Song of Songs is usually read on the Shabbat that falls in the middle of Pesach.

**Peshat:** The simple meaning of a verse or text.

**Petichah Petichot:** Literally, "a proem." Shabbat sermons were begun by introducing verses from the Prophets and Writings and then weaving them into the theme of the sermon. The act (and art) of doing this is called a *petichah.*

**Pikuach Nefesh:** Literally, "saving a life." The obligation to save a life supersedes all the commandments except the prohibitions against murder, idolatry, and sexual immorality.

**Pirkei Avot:** "Sayings of the Fathers." A tractate of the *Mishnah* that outlines the ethical teachings of many sages.

**Piyyut/Piyyutim:** Literally, "poetry." Liturgical poems.

**Prophets:** *Nevi'im* in Hebrew. The second section of the Bible, containing the books of Joshua, Judges, Samuel, Kings, Isaiah, Jeremiah, Ezekiel, and the Twelve Prophets.

**Proselyte:** A person who converts to Judaism. In Hebrew, a *ger* (male) or *gioret* (female).

**Purim:** Literally, "lots." The holiday that celebrates our deliverance from our enemy, Haman, by God, Esther, and Mordecai. The Book of Esther is read, and people exchange gifts of food, give *tsedakah* to the poor, and feast in observance of the day.

**Remez:** Literally, "a hint." The meaning hinted at in a biblical text. A method of biblical interpretation.

**Rosh Chodesh:** The first day (or two days) of a month. Rosh Chodesh is considered a kind of half-festival. *Hallel* is recited, but work may be done on this day.

**Sabbath:** Shabbat, in Hebrew. The seventh day of rest. The most holy day in the Jewish week.

**Sanhedrin:** The Great Sanhedrin. The court of seventy-one judges that met in Jerusalem and was ancient Israel's highest legislative body. It met in the Temple in Jerusalem.

**Scribes:** See *Sofrim.*

**Scriptures:** The Torah, Prophets, and Writings. Torah is considered to be directly, divinely revealed in traditional Judaism. Prophets and Writings are held to have a slightly lower level of holiness and authority.

**Sefer Torah/Sifrei Torah:** Literally, "a book of Torah." A Torah scroll.

**Sela:** A coin used in the talmudic era worth four *zuzim.*

**Shabbat/Shabbatot:** The seventh day of the week. A day of rest that lasts from Friday sundown to Saturday night.

**Shabbat Zachor:** See The Four Portions, above.

**Shavuot:** See Pentecost.

**Shechinah:** God's in-dwelling presence.

**Shehechiyanu:** That prayer said on all holidays and special occasions. "Blessed are You, *Adonai* our God, Ruler of the Universe, who has kept us alive, sustained us, and brought us to this time."

**Shirtut:** Lines made on a parchment by pressing a stylus into it. Torah scrolls, *mezuzuot*, religious divorce documents, and the *Megillah* require these lines.

**Shlach Manos:** See *Mishloach Manot*.

**Shoresh:** "Root." The three-letter core that each Hebrew word usually has.

**Simchah:** Literally, "happy." A happy event, such as the birth of a child, *bar* or *bat mitzvah*, or wedding.

**Sod:** Literally, "secret." The most hidden, mystical meaning of a biblical text.

**Sofrim:** Literally, "scribes." See Sages for more on the *Sofrim*.

**Sugyah/Sugyot:** A talmudic discussion. This word is derived from the verb "to go" in Aramaic. Thus a *sugyah* means literally "walking" or "passage."

**Sukkot:** The harvest festival of the fall. With this festival commence prayers for rain and the winter season. The Book of Ecclesiastes is usually read on the Shabbat in the middle of this festival.

**Tabernacles:** See Sukkot.

**Tadir v'she'eino tadir:** "Regularly/not regularly." A factor concerning ranking or ordering of *mitzvot*, prayers, etc.: Which comes more frequently? That which comes more frequently generally takes precedence over that which happens less frequently.

**Talmid Chacham:** Literally, "a wise student." A Torah sage.

**Tanach:** The Hebrew acronym for the Scriptures. **T**orah, **Ne**viim (Prophets), and **K**etuvim (Writings).

**Tanna/Tannaim:** A teacher of the Oral Law; one who recites *mishnayot*. The *Tannaim* are the sages of the Mishnaic period, 10–220 C.E.

**Targum:** The translation of the Bible into Aramaic.

**Tefillah/Tefillin:** "Phylacteries." Cube-shaped leather boxes that are tied to the hand and head. They contain the following passages written on parchment: Deuteronomy

6:4–9, Deuteronomy 11:13–21, Exodus 13:1–10, and Exodus 13:11–16.

**Tefillah/Tefillot:** "Prayer/prayers." Another name for the *Amidah* or *Shemoneh Esrei*. The prayer par excellence that is said three times each day.

**Terumah/Terumot:** The offering whose basis is Deuteronomy 18:4 and Numbers 18:12. This is an offering given to the priests from one's produce. It could be anywhere from one-fortieth to one-sixtieth of the total amount.

**Tisha B'Av:** Literally, "The Ninth of *Av*." This is the Jewish day of mourning for the destruction of both the First and Second Temples held on the ninth of the Jewish month of *Av*. The Book of Lamentations is read on this day.

**Torah:** The first five books of the Bible: Genesis, Exodus, Leviticus, Numbers, and Deuteronomy. Also a term designating Jewish learning in general.

**Toraitic:** From, or derived from, the first five books of the *Tanach*.

**Tosefta:** Literally, "addition" or "supplement." Tannaitic material collected into a compendium as an addition to the *Mishnah*. *Tosefta* does not have the authoritative stature of *mishnayot*.

**Tractate:** A volume of Talmud.

**Trope:** The song marks written into the biblical text that provide the tune to which the text is sung. They also function as punctuation. They are not found in the Torah scroll itself.

**Tsitsit:** The fringes on a *tallit*, a ritual prayer shawl, or on a four-cornered piece of cloth worn under the clothes as a fulfillment of the commandment in Numbers 15:37–41, which orders Jews to wear these fringes on the corners of their garments.

**Writings:** In Hebrew, *Ketuvim*. The third section of the *Tanach*, which contains the Psalms, Proverbs, Job, the Five Scrolls, Daniel, Ezra, Nehemia, and Chronicles.

**Yerushalmi:** The Talmud composed in the Land of Israel. It differs in many ways from the Babylonian Talmud and was completed in approximately 400 C.E.

**Yom Tov:** Literally, "a good day." A Jewish festival (Passover, Shavuot, etc.).

# For Further Reading

Blackman, Philip (1977). *Mishnayoth*. Gateshead: Judaica Press, Ltd. The *Mishnah* with vocalized Hebrew text, English translation, and notes. A useful tool for the beginning student.

Braude, William G. (1959). *Midrash on Psalms*. New Haven, CT: Yale University Press.

Bronstein, Herbert N., ed. (1984). *The Five Scrolls*. New York: C.C.A.R. An illustrated edition of the five scrolls, with introductions and liturgies reflecting a Reform Jewish standpoint.

Buchdahl, Gustav, Kushner, Lawrence, et al. *Ketubah*. Brookline, MA. An illuminated, egalitarian *ketubah*.

Carmell, Aryeh (1980). *Aids to Talmud Study*. New York: Feldheim. A useful reference work for beginning Talmud scholars.

Cowan, Paul, and Cowan, Rachel (1986). *A Torah is Written*. Philadelphia: Jewish Publication Society. Although this is a picture book intended for children, it is an instructive guide detailing the making of a Torah scroll from beginning to end.

*Encyclopaedia Judaica* (1972). Jerusalem: Keter Publishing House, Ltd.

Feldblum, Meyer S. (1964). "Prof. Abraham Weiss—His Approach and Contribution to Talmudic Scholarship," in *The Abraham Weiss Jubilee Volume*, pp. 7–81. New York: Yeshiva University. Abraham Weiss, a talmudic scholar who had a great grasp of how the Talmud was put together, wrote

151

his works in Hebrew. However, this is a good summary of
his insights in English.

Ginzberg, Louis. (1955). *On Jewish Law and Lore.* Philadelphia:
Jewish Publication Society. A very insightful look at the
development of Jewish law and the impact economic and
political events had on it. Marvelously written.

Goodblatt, David (1981). "The Babylonian Talmud." In *The
Study of Ancient Judaism, vol. II: The Palestinian and Babylonian Talmuds,* ed. Jacob Neusner, pp. 120–99. New York:
Ktav. A thorough review of the different theories regarding the Babylonian Talmud's composition.

Goodman, Philip (1973). *The Purim Anthology.* Philadelphia:
Jewish Publication Society.

Halivni, David Weiss (1974). *Sources and Traditions: A Source
Critical Commentary on the Talmud, Seder Moed from Yoma to
Hagiga.* New York: Jewish Theological Seminary. A tech-
nical, brilliant commentary tracing the development of
many *sugyot* in this, and other, tractates. Written in
Hebrew.

Harris, Lis (1985). *Holy Days: The World of a Hasidic Family.* New
York: MacMillan. A marvelous book describing traditional
Jewish life.

Heilman, Samuel (1984). *The Gate Behind the Wall: A Pilgrimage
to Jerusalem.* New York: Summit Books. A book about the
spiritual power of Talmud study.

Hertz, J. H., ed. (1960). *The Pentateuch and Haftorahs.* 2nd ed.
London: Soncino Press. Contains the Torah, *Haftarot,* and
commentaries from a traditional point of view.

*The Holy Scriptures* (1917). Philadelphia: Jewish Publication
Society.

Hyman, A. (1910). *Toledot Tanna'im ve-Amora'im.* Reprinted
1964. The classic work, in Hebrew describing the sages. A
reference work.

Jastrow, Marcus (1903). *A Dictionary of the Targumim, the Talmud
Babli and Yerushalmi, and the Midrashic Literature.* Israel. A
dictionary for those reading the Talmud in the original.

Kitov, Eliyahu (1978). *The Book of Our Heritage.* 3 vols. New
York: Philipp Feldheim, Inc. A good summary of the

history, theology, and practice of the Jewish holidays. Written from a traditional perspective.

Leiman, Sid Z. (1976). *The Canonization of Hebrew Scripture: The Talmudic and Midrashic Evidence.* Hamden, CT: Archon Books. A scholarly work on the processes behind the canonization of the *Tanach.* Contains many quotes in Hebrew and English from the rabbinic literature and an extensive bibliography on the topic.

Locks, Gutman G. (1985). *The Spice of Torah Gematria.* New York: Judaica Press.

Mielziner, Moses (1968). *Introduction to the Talmud.* New York: Bloch Publishing Company. A good basic reference work on the Talmud.

Neusner, Jacob, ed. (1970). *The Formation of the Babylonian Talmud.* Leiden, Netherlands: E. J. Brill. A more scholarly look at how the Talmud was composed. See chapters 7 and 8 (pp. 87–106) on Abraham Weiss and chapter 11 on David Weiss Halivni (pp. 134–74).

Neusner, Jacob (1981). *Tosefta: Moed, Second Division.* New York: Ktav.

Schauss, Hayyim (1938). *The Jewish Festivals from Their Beginnings to Our Own Day.* New York: U.A.H.C. A historical and anthropological summary of the origins of the Jewish holidays.

Seltzer, Robert M. (1980). *Jewish People, Jewish Thought: The Jewish Experience in History.* New York: MacMillan. A wonderful resource. A general history of Jewish life and thought.

Simon, Maurice (1948). *Tractate Megillah.* London: The Soncino Press.

Steinsaltz, Adin (1976). *The Essential Talmud.* New York: Basic Books. Steinsaltz is one of the greatest teachers of Talmud in this millennium.

Steinsaltz, Adin (1989). *The Talmud: The Steinsaltz Edition. A Reference Guide.* New York: Random House. An English translation of the Talmud with Steinsaltz's commentary. A masterpiece. The Reference Guide provides explanations of basic talmudic concepts and vocabulary.

Strack, H. L., and Stemberger, G. (1991). *Introduction to the Talmud and Midrash*. Edinburgh: T & T Clark. A technical reference work with many useful definitions and lists.

Strassfeld, Michael (1985). *The Jewish Holidays: A Guide and Commentary*. New York: Harper and Row. A guide to celebrating the Jewish holidays.

*Tanach* (1982). Philadelphia: Jewish Publication Society.

Zeitlin, Solomon (1933). *An Historical Study of the Canonization of the Hebrew Scriptures*. Philadelphia: Jewish Publication Society.

Zeitlin, Solomon (1950). "Jewish Apocryphal Literature," *Jewish Quarterly Review* 40:3 (January 1950): 223–257.

Zeitlin, Solomon (1968). *The Rise and Fall of the Judaean State*. 2 vols. Philadelphia: Jewish Publication Society. A thorough history of the history of the Second Commonwealth (332 B.C.E.–70 C.E.). He gives especially interesting insights into the political background of religious decisions.

# Index

—————— **About the Author** ——————

Judith Abrams is the rabbi of Congregation Beth El in Missouri City, Texas. A member of the Central Conference of American Rabbis Responsa Committee, she is the author of *The Talmud for Beginners, Volume I: Prayer, The Talmud for Beginners, Volume II: Text,* and several prayer books for children.